SHAPING THE FUTURE

MIDDLE SCHOOLS

Fanning/Howey
Associates, Inc.

IMPACT ON EDUCATION SERIES

This book is dedicated
to middle school students
in celebration of their
curiosity, energy, and spirit.

▽

Fanning/Howey Associates, Inc.
1200 Irmscher Boulevard
Celina, Ohio 45822
419/586-2292

We would like to thank the many school administrators, teachers, parents, students, and community members who assisted us in the research and development of *Shaping The Future: Middle Schools*. In publishing our series of books on the impact of facility design on the quality of education, we have talked with hundreds of people who have shared their insights and experiences regarding school buildings—including nearly 200 for this book. We hope that their observations and comments, along with our own experience in working with school districts, will be helpful to all who read this.

In particular, we would like to thank the participants of our focus groups:

Metropolitan School District of Pike Township

Lincoln Middle School; Indianapolis, Indiana
February 2, 1998

Bill Gigowski, *Seventh-Grade Student*
Ryan Gralia, *Sixth-Grade Student*
Heather Guzman, *Seventh-Grade Student*
Doug Kriech, *Seventh-Grade Student*
Ashley Magee, *Seventh-Grade Student*
Aubrey Mullins, *Seventh-Grade Student*
Sabrina Patterson, *Sixth-Grade Student*
Nathaniel Patty, *Sixth-Grade Student*
Erica Lynne Starks, *Sixth-Grade Student*
Trey Winfrey, *Seventh-Grade Student*
Steven Andzer, *Sixth-Grade Teacher*
Deborah Crutchfield, *Sixth-Grade Teacher*
Karlyn Fox, *Sixth-Grade Teacher*

Deb Hornaday, *Sixth-Grade Teacher*
Janet Karsas, *Sixth-Grade Teacher*
Debbie Meloy, *Sixth-Grade Teacher*
Andy Ohmer, *Sixth-Grade Teacher*
Leila Peters, *Sixth-Grade Teacher*
Jennifer Powers, *Sixth-Grade Teacher*
Maggie Rice, *Sixth-Grade Teacher*
Susan Sanders, *Sixth-Grade Teacher*
Virgil Taueg, *Principal*
Kathryn Vetarbo, *Student Teacher*

South Vermillion Community School Corporation

South Vermillion Middle School;
Clinton, Indiana
February 3, 1998

Connie Adams, *Eighth-Grade Teacher*

Kim Bruce, *Life Skills Teacher*

David Harris, *Principal*

Charles Jackson, *Seventh-Grade Teacher*

Dale Orman, *Art Teacher*

Linda Underwood, *Counselor*

Linda Whiteman, *Eighth-Grade Teacher*

Aptakisic-Tripp Community Consolidated School District No. 102

Meridian Middle School; Buffalo Grove, Illinois

February 3, 1998

Max Chiswick, *Sixth-Grade Student*

Timmy Chmielewski, *Fifth-Grade Student*

Andrew Conner, *Fifth-Grade Student*

Jenna Green, *Fifth-Grade Student*

Stefanie Herst, *Sixth-Grade Student*

Samantha LeVine, *Sixth-Grade Student*

Blair Lewin, *Sixth-Grade Student*

Ian Ludwig, *Fifth-Grade Student*

Jeremy Rose, *Sixth-Grade Student*

Brittany Sarmas, *Fifth-Grade Student*

Alex Yastrow, *Fifth-Grade Student*

Barbara Young, *Fifth-Grade Student*

Jan Benkoske, *Art Teacher*

Sharon Borg, *Sixth-Grade Teacher*

Sherrie Cummins, *Fifth-Grade Teacher*

Students at Meridian Middle School in Buffalo Grove, Illinois, were among focus group participants for Shaping The Future: Middle Schools.

Wendy Friedman, *Fifth-Grade Teacher*

Susan Mann, *Principal*

Barry Nagle, *Sixth-Grade Teacher*

Cathy Rosen, *Adapted P.E. Teacher*

Debbie Roycroft, *Sixth-Grade Teacher*

Jean Sweeney, *Student Success Coordinator*

MaryJo Taylor, *Media Center Director*

Marianne Todd, *Building Secretary*

Mike Williams, *Technology Director*

Penn-Harris-Madison School Corporation

Discovery Middle School; Granger, Indiana

February 4, 1998

Eddie Beebe, *Seventh-Grade Student*

SHAPING THE FUTURE
Middle Schools

Teddy Bradley, *Seventh-Grade Student*

Jillian Frick, *Eighth-Grade Student*

Nancy LaDuke, *Seventh-Grade Student*

Michelle Long, *Seventh-Grade Student*

Colette Miller, *Sixth-Grade Student*

Amanda Piekarski, *Sixth-Grade Student*

Chad Rajski, *Eighth-Grade Student*

Tim Braunsdorf, *Seventh-Grade Teacher*

Sheryll Harper, *Principal*

Diane Keller, *Media Specialist*

Jim Pattison, *Tech Aide*

Matt Reininga, *Sixth-Grade Teacher*

Jon Robinson, *Head Custodian*

Chuck Sowders, *Seventh-Grade Teacher*

Mitzie Thornton, *Seventh-Grade Substitute Teacher*

Sheila Toth, *Fitness Teacher*

Elaine Truex, *Secretary*

Keely Twibell, *Seventh-Grade Teacher*

Metropolitan School District of Steuben County

Angola Middle School; Angola, Indiana
February 4, 1998

Wes Bickford, *Seventh-Grade Student*

Boyd Jackson, *Sixth-Grade Student*

Ruben Ryan, *Seventh-Grade Student*

Leah Seevers, *Eighth-Grade Student*

Chelsea Thiebaut, *Eighth-Grade Student*

Beau Vincent, *Sixth-Grade Student*

Beth Weber, *Eighth-Grade Student*

Paul Beckwith, *Seventh-Grade Teacher*

Bill Church, *Principal*

Deborah Gilbert, *Eighth-Grade Teacher*

Dean Harter, *Sixth-Grade Teacher*

Gary Kearney, *Seventh-Grade Teacher*

Joe Kennedy, *Eighth-Grade Teacher*

David McKinney, *Health Teacher*

Brant Moore, *Music Teacher*

Mark Ridenour, *Assistant Principal/Athletic Director*

Penny Snyder, *Sixth-Grade Teacher*

Medina City Schools

A.I. Root Middle School; Medina, Ohio
February 12, 1998

Jeremy Abraham, *Eighth-Grade Student*

Whitney Byrd, *Eighth-Grade Student*

Megan Flanagan, *Eighth-Grade Student*

Jon Hanwell, *Eighth-Grade Student*

Debbie Bock, *Home Economics Teacher*

Tess Ewart, *Eighth-Grade Teacher*

Jane Langol, *Aide, Handicapped Program*

Tom McKenna, *Principal*

Mike Pallini, *Associate Principal*

Tonya Stanfar, *Consulting Teacher*

Barb Steingass, *Media Specialist*

Fairfax County Public Schools

Edgar Allan Poe Middle School;

Annandale, Virginia

February 19, 1998

Mary Artz, *Eighth-Grade Teacher*

Sheila Chenard, *Eighth-Grade Teacher*

Michael Eckhoff, *Assistant Director, Design & Construction; Fairfax County Public Schools*

Bill Hirst, *Seventh-Grade Teacher*

Betsy Lockman, *Sixth-Grade Teacher*

June Monterio, *Principal*

Louise Morello, *Eighth-Grade Teacher and Department Chair*

James Shepherd, *Seventh-Grade Teacher*

A special *thank you* goes to Joy Kelly at Edgar Allan Poe Middle School, who helped us in more ways than we can count—including coordinating the photography of the Poe students who appear in the chapter title pages and throughout the book.

Architecture is both a technology and an art. It must meet both instrumental and aesthetic needs. A building must be useful for the purpose for which it is designed as well as attractive to those who enter it and even to those who just drive by.

When designing a school, an architect and his or her clients (the school system) must have in mind the needs of the instructional program and the other needs (for security and management, for instance) of operating a middle school today and in the future. These needs are many and detailed, including such things as locker placement; proximity of classrooms, labs, and libraries; wiring for technology; and cafeteria/auditorium design. But the entire design also needs to work as a whole—as an environment in which the instructional program works for youngsters, teachers, and others in the school. Neither the details nor the whole can dominate the design.

Middle schools offer a special challenge to architects. The students who attend these schools are at an age at which they are especially impressionable, adventurous, and experimental. Middle school teachers know how to channel these traits into learning. The school's design can be critical to the teachers' effectiveness. Over the past several years, middle school organization and pedagogy have developed more than at any other grade level. For instance, cross-disciplinary team teaching has become common in middle schools, and sixth grades are more commonly included in middle schools. The physical organization of the school can contribute to or hinder these developments. Good design can make a big difference.

Middle school students have special needs to feel secure and be recognized as individuals, which the new developments in middle school pedagogy help fulfill, as well as needs for academic learning. School design can also help students feel secure and valued as individuals.

The aesthetic component of education is especially important for middle school students. A beautiful school sends an important message to youngsters at this age. It is a message that their school—and their society—care about them and that beauty is an important value. Students are more likely to work hard and succeed in a beautiful building.

A useful and beautiful middle school can be designed from the ground up or as a renovation of an existing building. As superintendent of the Fairfax County Public Schools, I have seen both. This year, we opened a new school with all the features for an excellent middle school program. Included in this book is the renovation of Edgar Allen Poe Middle School, a new/old school that provides useful and beautiful space for students and teachers.

Architecture is a very important component of any school's program. The administrator who makes sure that design and construction meet the utilitarian and aesthetic needs of students and teachers goes a long way toward ensuring a successful school.

—Dr. Daniel A. Domenech, Superintendent, Fairfax County Public Schools, Virginia
    President, American Association of School Administrators

Halfway through each school year, Joe Kennedy, a language arts teacher at Angola Middle School in Angola, Indiana, asks his students what they think they have learned so far. According to Kennedy, the nature of many of the responses has changed since the school fully implemented teaming two years ago—he now hears more comments such as, "I actually learned that a teacher can be my friend and someone I can trust—that's what I've learned this year."

Ask a teacher at the middle school level about priorities, and he or she will most likely talk about educating the *whole* student—in other words, going beyond the academic basics and helping to shape the student's emotional, social, and physical development as well. Adolescence is a critical age in the educational process, when a child's appetite for learning can either be greatly nourished or lost forever. By working in teams—planning together, comparing notes, exchanging and building upon ideas, sharing concerns, and *collaborating*—teachers are able to mentor students effectively and create compelling educational experiences. Inspiring and enriching a young student's mind may require trying many different types of approaches—what may not work for one student may be just the right approach to reach another.

While vastly rewarding, teaching at the middle school level is truly challenging work. For this reason, teachers are often quick to praise new or modernized school environments that facilitate the educational program. Buildings should support the educational mission and enhance—rather than inhibit—learning opportunities. Our experience tells us that the best school buildings are created when, as architects and engineers, we do our own form of teaming: interactive planning and design, in which we work in collaboration with teachers and administrators to develop optimal learning environments.

– Fanning/Howey Associates, Inc.

THE MORNING SCRAMBLE

"IT'S IMPORTANT TO HAVE A NICE SCHOOL BECAUSE IT'S KIND OF LIKE A HOME AWAY FROM HOME. AT SCHOOL YOU SHOULD FEEL COMFORTABLE AND NOT AFRAID."

—Alex Yastrow, Fifth-Grade Student, Meridian Middle School; Buffalo Grove, Illinois

BEFORE-SCHOOL ACTIVITIES
M/W/F 7:30-8:40

EXPLORERS CLASS (HOME BASE)
M/T/W/TH/F 8:50-9:10

Bells start ringing early in the morning at Lincoln Middle School in Indianapolis, Indiana—but not school bells. Three times a week, starting at 7:30 a.m., the 15-student handbell choir meets for practice in the choral room. Over in the academic wing of the school, a morning French class gathers every other day in the distance learning center, where the students participate in interactive sessions hosted by another school. Many students also come early for breakfast—meeting every morning in the auditeria to eat, talk, catch up on homework, and scan the large monitors that greet them with schedule updates and school news.

"When I first get here in the morning, it's quiet—but that doesn't last long," says Principal Virgil Taueg. "The students start arriving by 7:30 for before-school clubs and activities. Then the cars and buses start rolling in, phones start ringing, and kids head in all different directions. The building just comes to life."

Welcoming hundreds of students in the morning is never a small task for teachers and administrators. Lobbies, commons areas, and hallways fill quickly with children as they rush to meet with friends, visit lockers, and hurry to class. "It's the busiest time of day," says Taueg. "While the students are pouring in, the phones are ringing with parents reporting absences and appointments, and we're also working with our substitutes on the classes they'll cover. Teachers are checking their mailboxes, voicemail, and e-mail, and then greeting the students."

The chaotic atmosphere is fun for many children, but can be intimidating or distracting for others—especially younger students. Making their way to class in the morning can lead to frayed nerves and frustration on the part of new students, especially at the beginning of the school year. The size of the facility alone may make students uneasy: middle school buildings are typically larger and less compact than elementary schools, housing more students and offering a greater number of specialized program areas. Lockers are also a new experience for most middle-school students, requiring organization and quick thinking between classes in order to be prepared with books, assignments, and other materials.

Rather than school bells, the bell choir can be heard early in the morning at Lincoln Middle School in Indianapolis, Indiana.

"When I first came here, I thought I was going to get lost," says Erica Lynne Starks, a sixth-grade student at Lincoln Middle School. "But when I saw that all of the sixth-grade classes were in the same area, that helped." Completed in 1997 to replace a turn-of-the-century building, Lincoln's new academic area is organized into grade-level pods, with each pod accommodating two "teams" of teachers and students. "It's better than the old school because we don't have to travel so far to get from class to class," says Starks. "I know some people that had to go from the basement to the second floor in the old building. It's easier between classes because we don't have to rush around so much. All of our classes are in this one big area."

Lincoln Middle School students meet before school with pen pals from nearby Hamilton Southeastern Junior High School. Members of the Lincoln Middle School Junior Venture Club also meet before classes start.

While most elementary schools build educational programs around "self-contained" classrooms, allowing primary school students to remain with one teacher throughout much of the day, middle schools typically offer a more flexible, interdisciplinary approach to curricula in which students move throughout several classrooms, working in teams. This transition often represents the most significant change for students as they begin middle school. Organization of the building itself can make a critical difference in facilitating the team instructional approach, while also easing the apprehensions of students as they attempt to feel comfortable in their new environment.

THE MORNING SCRAMBLE

"It's nice here because of the way the different grades are divided up," says Doug Kriech, a seventh-grade student at Lincoln Middle School. As a sixth-grader at the "old Lincoln," Kriech found that getting to class could be a challenge: "The hallways weren't very well organized, and they were so packed that you got pushed down the stairs and you ran into other people."

"Before our new school was built, my team wasn't even on the same level," says Linda Whiteman, an eighth-grade math teacher at South Vermillion Middle School in Clinton, Indiana. The school opened in 1995 to replace a long-outdated school originally built in 1919. "Plus, we had kids in the basement when their lockers were on the top floor. Now, the lockers are right outside our rooms, and we can say to kids, 'Don't forget that book,' or, 'Do you have your assignment?' and everything's accessible."

The South Vermillion Community School Corporation, like many school districts around the country, fully embraced a teaming approach when it moved to its new building. "We went from being a traditional junior high school to the team concept," says Connie Adams, an eighth-grade English teacher at South Vermillion Middle School. "We work together with a core of academic teachers sharing the same group of students and planning their whole day. Whereas before, each teacher was locked in with the students without interaction with other classes. The students were just like a herd of cattle."

The most successful middle school buildings, according to Dr. William S. DeJong, an educational facilities planner, accommodate all types of delivery systems in education, including teaming, self-contained instruction, a departmental approach, multi-age grouping, and looping—in which the same teacher or group of teachers follows students from one grade level to the next. "The building should never dictate the delivery system," says Dr. DeJong. "It should be flexible enough to accommodate each type of approach, or a combination."

Dr. DeJong points to the team approach as the most prevalent in middle schools today—and the approach most likely to shape the future of education. "The teaming concept has become the mainstay of educational approaches at the middle school level," he says. "Teaming is a driving force in curriculum development, and ultimately it will impact elementary and high school education as well because it's the most student-centered of all approaches—it puts students first."

"When we first moved in, we brought all the kids on our team to the large-group instruction room," says Gary Kearney, a science and geography teacher at Angola Middle School in Angola, Indiana, which was recently expanded and renovated—in part to accommodate teaming. "We introduced ourselves and said to the kids, 'We're one family here—and we're all going to get to know each other.'"

Joe Kennedy, a language arts teacher at Angola Middle School, confirms that the teaming concept has brought teachers closer to the students since it was fully implemented in 1996, following completion of the facility modernization: "Every year—about halfway through the year—I ask my students what they have learned in class so far. And the last two years I've gotten a lot more comments like, 'Well, I actually learned that a teacher can be my friend and someone I can trust—that's what I've learned this year.' And they've learned it because of the way we're teaching now. It's not just 'Okay, let's go open a book and learn from it.' It's different. It's a sense of community."

A colorful mural, glassed-in display space, and an attractive main office suite welcome students and visitors at South Vermillion Middle School. The school's carpeting, which reflects the colors chosen for each of the three grade-level pods, is a favorite among teachers: "The hallway noise was really bad at the old school," says Connie Adams, an eighth-grade English teacher. "Here, with the carpeting, it's so quiet you can walk down the hall and sneak up on people!"

The corridors at Central Junior High School in West Melbourne, Florida, are colorful and brightly lighted, and are wide enough to accommodate circulation and locker visits. Stacked lockers save space (and may be more appropriate to warmer climates where heavy coats aren't often needed), although they may result in increased locker congestion.

WHAT SIZE SHOULD THE LOCKERS BE?

Ask a student who's just about to enter middle school about his or her biggest fear, and the answer will often be, "I'm afraid the older kids will stuff me in my locker!" Concerns about lockers—including not being able to manage the lock and get into them, as well as keeping *out* of them if bullies threaten—are common at nearly every middle school.

Locker headaches persist for teachers and administrators as well. In planning new locker areas, issues include: the size of the locker—including width and height (generally: big enough for coats, backpacks, and large books, but too small for children's bodies); and the arrangement—typically either along hallways or clustered within small commons areas near classrooms. Ease of access, noise control, and supervision are key factors in determining the configuration and location of locker areas.

"I like to see the lockers clustered within the academic pod areas," says Walt Grebing, president of the National Middle School Association and an educational program consultant. "That helps in accommodating a flexible block scheduling program. I would also avoid having lockers along major corridors with a lot of traffic. And each student should have a locker—locker 'partners' don't always work."

Most lockers, such as these at Angola Middle School in Angola, Indiana, are made of metal. Metal lockers can be refurbished over time, and color schemes can be changed.

Many lockers have flat tops, enabling students to store books and other material temporarily during locker visits. As alternatives, lockers also come with sloped tops, or they can be set into the corridor walls—such as these at Williamsburg Middle/High School in Williamsburg, Ohio. These options eliminate the potential for litter accumulation.

Manufacturers today issue lockers at a size that easily accommodates backpacks (usually at least 12 inches deep and 12 inches wide)—an option for school administrators who prefer that students not carry backpacks from class to class.

Most lockers feature built-in, durable locks; shelves for books; and hooks for coats and backpacks. The units are typically available in a variety of paint colors, so that lockers can become an integral part of pod or grade-level color coding, or reflect school colors.

Do kids really get shoved into lockers, and are the students' fears valid? "We want every student to feel that the school is a safe environment," says Dr. Bernie Gross, principal of Cooper Middle School in McLean, Virginia. "The lockers are a big concern to them. We spend time during the first few days of school helping them practice with their locks, and we're constantly supervising the hallways. The idea that students get pushed into lockers is a big rumor that circulates every year, but it doesn't happen here."

One Cooper Middle School seventh-grade student offers her own account: "When I first saw our lockers, I thought they could fit a very small person, but it would be a lot of work to try to get someone in there. I'm tall so I didn't worry. The only kid I ever saw being stuffed in a locker was actually stuffing himself in the locker to see if he could do it!"

LINCOLN MIDDLE SCHOOL; INDIANAPOLIS, INDIANA

"We are constantly learning how to use this building in different ways," says Principal Virgil Taueg of Lincoln Middle School. "Between the building itself and the technology, we have so many more opportunities than we did in our old school."

Completed in 1997 to replace an aging structure that no longer accommodated the Metropolitan School District of Pike Township's middle school instructional program, the new Lincoln Middle School is flexibly designed to support a number of educational approaches—including teaming. Each grade has its own wing, with classrooms organized around a commons space. The wings also have their own large-group instruction room, conference rooms, and teacher planning areas. Color coding each wing—in blue, green, or burgundy—contributes to the grade-level identity.

"I've taught in a number of middle schools and it's hard to team unless it's designed like this," says Jennifer Powers, a sixth-grade English teacher. "With the grade-level pods, teams have their own space. We can do things in our own hallway that the students see every day. Before, we were so spread out that there wasn't any central space that was ours. Now we can have an 'Olympian' hallway, or a 'Voyager' hallway for the teams. The students know where they belong."

The teachers at Lincoln Middle School also attribute improved student supervision to the layout of the school. "You know the children who are in your area," says Susan Sanders, a sixth-grade computer instructor. "The students you are supervising in the hall are the students you have in class—this makes for more effective discipline." Karlyn Fox, a sixth-grade math teacher, adds, "The organization of the academic wing keeps the

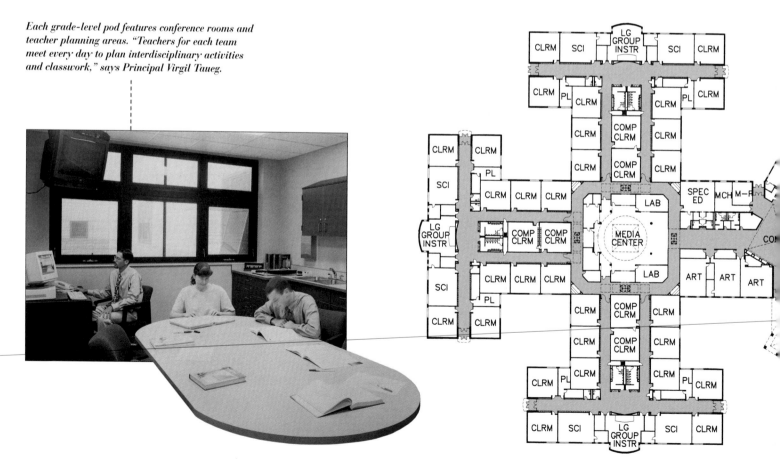

Each grade-level pod features conference rooms and teacher planning areas. "Teachers for each team meet every day to plan interdisciplinary activities and classwork," says Principal Virgil Taueg.

The auditeria at Lincoln Middle School sees frequent use by students and the community. The room starts to fill before 8:00 a.m. with students arriving for breakfast each morning.

LINCOLN MIDDLE SCHOOL; INDIANAPOLIS, INDIANA

Students studying French at Lincoln Middle School participate in an early morning distance learning program that enables them to interact with classes from other schools in the Metropolitan School District of Pike Township.

Students claim to feel much more at home at the new Lincoln Middle School, where they no longer have to negotiate stairs and narrow hallways. The building's exterior features a landscaped plaza that connects the main entry with the public entry near the gym.

Each morning, Lincoln Middle School airs a news program written and produced by students. The "studio" is housed in a room adjacent to the school's media center in the academic portion of the building.

LINCOLN MIDDLE SCHOOL

The spacious commons at Lincoln Middle School welcomes students and the community. The commons area links the public realm of the building with the academic realm, and is used for a variety of gatherings, including town meetings.

sixth-graders away from the eighth-graders, and that's good. There can be a big difference between students in the sixth and eighth grades, and we need to keep them separate."

Taueg cites staff and student communication as one aspect that has changed dramatically in the new building. "We rarely interrupt classes for announcements—all they have to do is look up at the monitors to find out what's going on. I also think it's an asset that they need to *read* this information." Taueg regularly relies on e-mail to communicate with staff: "Most mornings, the teachers have some sort of greeting or announcement from me—usually a 'Did You Know?' type of message. I can also forward information directly from the superintendent's office."

The communications program at Lincoln Middle School also encompasses a student-run morning video news program. Students can "catch the news" each morning in their "Explorers Class," beginning at 8:50. "We designed the Explorers Class to give the students a home base," says Taueg. "It gives them some continuity throughout the year. We use the time for brief activities and to watch the news program." Written, presented, and produced by the students, the morning news program typically runs seven or eight minutes, reviewing schedule highlights and bringing attention to student achievements. "It's a big deal to be on the news here," says Taueg. "And the language arts and media aspects of producing the news are an important part of the students' classwork."

"I hardly even use paper to communicate anymore," Taueg notes. "The technology here is great. Everything about this building has enhanced our program—our ability to team, communicate, expand student activities, involve parents, and bring in the community. Does this building make a difference? It's like night and day."

The new Williamsburg Middle/High School in Williamsburg, Ohio, accommodates 700 students in grades 6-12. General classrooms for the middle school students are clustered near a separate main entry, away from the high school wing of the building.

A landscaped plaza with seating welcomes students and visitors to Hamilton Southeastern Junior High School in Fishers, Indiana. The plaza adjoins the main entry, as well as entries to the academic and public wings of the building.

A large commons area at Hamilton Southeastern Junior High School offers access to the main office, and separates the public realm of the building from the academic realm.

The courtyard at Central Junior High School serves as a gathering place for students before and after school. In addition to providing an informal environment for social interaction, the courtyard is sized for large events, including stage presentations, pep rallies, and dances.

Central Junior High School in West Melbourne, Florida, accommodates 1,650 students. The school is designed around an enclosed courtyard. "Student safety is a top priority," says Dr. David E. Sawyer, superintendent of the School Board of Brevard County. "We are building more courtyard-type schools at the middle school and elementary school levels, rather than campus-style schools."

Leapin' Lizards, Raptors, And The Brainy Bunch

"MIDDLE SCHOOLS
ARE WHERE WE NEED
OUR VERY BEST
TEACHERS—AND OUR
VERY BEST BUILDINGS."

—*Judith A. Cochran, Ph.D.,*
E. Desmond Lee Endowed
Professor of Education,
University of Missouri,
St. Louis

LEAPIN' LIZARDS, RAPTORS, AND THE BRAINY BUNCH

LANGUAGE ARTS
M/T/W/F 9:15-10:05, TH 9:15-11:00

"We want students to be able to make *connections* in their studies," says Dr. Richard N. Clapp, superintendent of the Woodridge Local School District in Cuyahoga Falls, Ohio. "It's especially important for middle school students to understand the relationship between subjects—how being able to write well can help them with their science experiments, for example. Our teachers work in teams and talk daily about interdisciplinary lessons and coordinating work for the students."

"Curriculum is integrative when it helps students make sense out of their life experiences. This requires curriculum that is itself coherent, that helps students connect school experiences to their daily lives outside the school, and that encourages them to reflect on the totality of their experiences."

—THIS WE BELIEVE, NATIONAL MIDDLE SCHOOL ASSOCIATION

Like many school districts around the country, Woodridge Local School District has embraced a middle school philosophy that includes grade-level teaming and the use of integrated curriculum. "An integrated curriculum enables a child to think in a global way, rather than linear," says Dr. Judith Cochran, Ph.D., professor of education at the University of Missouri, St. Louis. Dr. Cochran, who specializes in training middle school teachers, advocates an approach that encourages students to look for relationships, or connections, between subject areas. "In language arts, for example," Dr. Cochran says, "a child doesn't simply think 'first we'll do spelling, then we'll do reading, and then we'll do writing'. With an integrated curriculum, learning is often more topical. Students might study water, for example. They can read about water, write about rivers, study ice in science, and explore water in several different academic subject areas."

The sixth-grade "Voyag team at Lincoln Mic School in Indianapc Indiana, embarked or ambitious interdisciplin instructional unit in January 1 focusing on the *Titanic*. Accorc to Maggie Rice, the Voyager tea English teacher and organizer of *Titanic* unit, the program span several days and made use of all different sixth-grade disciplines. "On the benefits of being in a building like th that you have the space to take on projects," Rice says. "Every day we sent students who were in 'first class' to

Such broad-ranging, collaborative study programs typically require spacious, flexible facilities. "Our teachers were very involved with the design of Woodridge Middle School," says Dr. Clapp. "They knew that each grade needed to have its own wing, and that teams needed to be kept together. They wanted to be able to work with all of the students in one grade in a large group, or in smaller groups as needed—so they wanted space that would give them a lot of flexibility. Now students have their own wing, with their own set of teachers. It's their home base, where they spend most of the day. And with teachers collaborating more, the students don't feel bombarded. Everything is coordinated. I believe that teachers are better able to help students with their social and emotional development as well."

When students at Lincoln Middle School in Indianapolis, Indiana, studied the *Titanic*, instructional activities and hands-on projects were held throughout the school—including classrooms and science labs, large-group instruction areas, commons spaces, hallways, and the media center. "The entire team planned the *Titanic* unit together," says Principal Virgil Taueg. "The project involved language arts, social studies, science, reading, computers, math—teachers met every day on this. On the 'big day', we set up the lifeboat stations in the classrooms. When the 'abandon ship' order was given, first-class students were released to get life preservers from their lockers. 'Steerage' students were held several minutes past the 'abandon ship.' We studied the evacuation process—and really looked at the emotional side of it—the human side. In the end, of course, some students made it to lifeboat stations and some didn't."

he large-group
ruction area. The
dents who were the 'crew'
ved them. We used the
ker areas, the LGI, and
eral classrooms during the
cuation process; and the
ncipal was able to make the call to
andon ship" over the intercom,
ch was only broadcast to our area. As
ship was sinking, we had our handbell
ir playing in the commons outside the
I. The kids loved it all, and because we
roached the topic through a lot of
erent subjects and teaching styles, they
e able to learn much more."

"If a building is not designed to fit a middle school program, it's like trying to fit a square peg into a round hole. It's not ideal for the kids. At our new school, teaming concepts and an integrated curriculum will be emphasized."

—Dr. Marc Crail,
Superintendent, Kent City
Schools, Ohio

DISCARD

LEAPIN' LIZARDS, RAPTORS, AND THE BRAINY BUNCH

With media centers now playing a more integral role in school-wide curriculum, media specialists often work hand-in-hand with teachers to help carry out special projects and activities. Eighth-grade language arts students at Chester Middle School in Chester, Virginia, recently used a variety of library materials to do follow-up research about the Holocaust after reading *Anne Frank: Diary of a Young Girl*. Another team studied poets and used the media center for a "Poets' Tea," while students in the school's health classes studied nutrition using library resources. Other topics recently explored in the media center—using the Internet, CD-ROMs, and printed materials—have included classical musicians, inventors, and the Vietnam War. "Librarians don't just stand at the desk," says Anne Sutton, head librarian at Chester Middle School. "We constantly interact with students and teachers. As a result, we need space to teach, host special events, create displays and contest areas, and store a variety of materials."

Media centers at the middle school level now see constant use by students and faculty, rather than the "once a week" visit by classes that was more typical in the past. "Our teachers have kids in and out of the media center all day long," says Dr. Clapp. "It's accessible from all the grade-level wings, and teachers use it daily. Students use it constantly for instruction and research. Going to the media center is no longer an 'event'—it's a vital part of the program."

Media centers at the middle school level are often as large as 4,000 to 5,000 square feet, enabling two or three classes to visit at the same time. The facility is used more frequently for formal instruction as well, as opposed to independent reading and research assignments only. Small conference rooms, offices, production areas, computer labs and reading nooks positioned around the perimeter of the main reference room facilitate small-group discussions and related instructional activities. Often, media centers are a central part of a school's computer network, allowing students and faculty to access resources from their classrooms or even from home.

Clearly, media centers have evolved beyond book-based learning, to encompass computer research and assignments, multimedia presentations and production activities, small- and large-group discussions, hands-on demonstrations, and interactive displays. "Our media center fits our philosophy," says Sheryll Harper, principal of Discovery Middle School in Granger, Indiana. "It's very conducive to collaboration. We wanted it to be very flexible and accommodating to a lot of different activities."

Still, books remain at the heart of the media center and its mission. "I'm trying to create a reading culture here—that's my guiding philosophy," says Sutton. Like many media specialists, she strives to preserve student interest in books in the face of growing competition from sophisticated multimedia technology—ranging from educational computer programs to video games. To encourage reading, Sutton sponsors authors' "Book Talks," daily almanac contests, and a host of competitions in which students accumulate reading points. "We want to immerse our students in books," Sutton says. "I want to see a love of reading throughout the building."

WOODRIDGE MIDDLE SCHOOL; PENINSULA, OHIO

Two primary objectives drove the planning and design process for the new Woodridge Middle School in Peninsula, Ohio: accommodating a variety of instructional delivery methods, and providing wide-ranging student and teacher access to technology and diverse informational tools. These goals were met with the completion of the 550-student, 80,000-square-foot school, where efforts to maximize long-term building flexibility yielded a versatile yet efficient layout that promotes collaborative learning and team teaching.

"This school was planned to fit a middle school philosophy," says Dr. Richard N. Clapp, superintendent of the Woodridge Local School District. Dr. Clapp points to the involvement of the school's principal and several teachers as being critical to the success of the design: "We wanted clusters for each grade, and the ability to gather students in one space, or divide teams in half, or in smaller groups. We wanted flexibility and to be able to accommodate future growth."

For Dr. Clapp, an unexpected attribute of the school is its tranquil atmosphere.

Areas that house noisier activities—such as the gym, the cafeteria, and the industrial technology lab—are located in the public realm of the building, away from classrooms. "There are many times during the day that you wouldn't even know that kids were there," he says. "If you're near the classrooms, you will hear the 'learning noises'. But in

Set in the midst of Ohio's Cuyahoga Valley National Recreational Area, Woodridge Middle School enjoys a wooded site. Classroom clusters are arranged to maximize views of the woods. Clerestory windows in an elevated alcove above the media center bring in natural daylight and demarcate the hub of the academic clusters of the school.

general it's very peaceful."

The core academic zones of the award-winning school encircle a 4,000-square-foot media center—the interior and exterior focal point of the building and the "hub" of the school, according to Dr. Clapp. The school's floor plan takes its cue from a child's pin-wheel, with the academic clusters radiating from the media center.

Clerestory windows illuminate the media center with natural daylight and create a beacon effect when lit in the evening.

Woodridge Middle School is set in the heart of the Cuyahoga Valley National Recreational Area, just south of Cleveland. Much of the woodland area was preserved on the site, and the school's brick and cast stone exterior complements its natural setting. But despite its attractive exterior, the real success story lies on the inside of the building: "It works even better than we anticipated," says Dr. Clapp. "The teachers love it, and the students are proud of it."

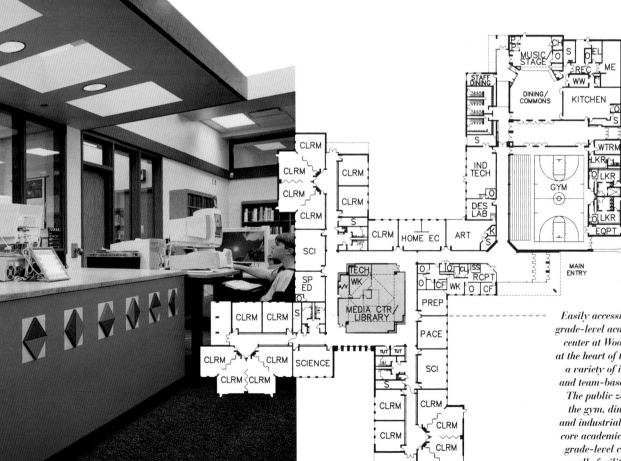

Easily accessible from each of the three grade-level academic clusters, the media center at Woodridge Middle School lies at the heart of the facility and is used for a variety of independent, small-group, and team-based instructional activities. The public zone of the building houses the gym, dining/commons area, stage, and industrial technology lab; while the core academic clusters contain separate grade-level classroom areas. Operable walls facilitate team and large-group activities in the classroom areas.

CHALLENGE

A DAY AT THE BEACH

Join the Accelerated Reader Program, and earn points for every book you read from the media center. At year-end, the 50 students with the highest number of points will receive gift certificates to a local bookstore, and be invited to a special pizza party. Earn pencils and trading cards along the way. If 50,000 points are accumulated school-wide by the end of the year, your librarians will host a "Day At The Beach" party and wear "gay nineties" bathing suits for an entire day...

The large-group instruction room at South Vermillion Middle School in Clinton, Indiana, sees frequent use for classes, awards ceremonies, and performances.

—HIGHLIGHTS OF THE ACCELERATED READER PROGRAM AT CHESTER MIDDLE SCHOOL IN CHESTER, VIRGINIA. IN PAST COMPETITIONS, LIBRARIANS AND TEACHERS HAVE DONNED BATHING SUITS, CLIMBED ONTO THE SCHOOL'S ROOF, AND EVEN HAD THEIR HEADS SHAVED TO CELEBRATE STUDENT ACHIEVEMENTS IN READING.

"In our old school, we were so crammed in our classrooms," says Connie Adams, an eighth-grade English teacher at South Vermillion Middle School. *"Now we have space to move around, and to move furniture around as we need to."*

The academic wing of Discovery Middle School houses three grade levels in separate "neighborhoods." Each neighborhood accommodates two teams of up to 150 students. Perimeter cabinetry and storage areas reduce clutter in the center of the classrooms, enabling students and teachers to move about more freely.

"People come into this room and just say 'Wow!'" says Diane Keller, a media specialist at Discovery Middle School in Granger, Indiana. The center includes a spacious reading/reference area, computer classroom, conference room, work technology area, production room for video editing, and two resource rooms.*

"The difference between our old media center and the new one here is like night and day," says Charles Jackson, a seventh-grade science teacher at South Vermillion Middle School. *"The new media center is used a lot more—for reading, research, computer instruction, and just a quiet place to go."*

The media center at North Oldham Middle School in Goshen, Kentucky, includes offices, a conference room, a reading room, and a multi-purpose room. The reading room also opens into a landscaped courtyard at the center of the school. The center is sized and configured to accommodate a variety of independent, small-group, and large-group activities.

LEAPIN' LIZARDS, RAPTORS, AND THE BRAINY BUNCH

Oak furniture in the media center at Lincoln Middle School in Indianapolis, Indiana, facilitates computer-based research. The tables and desks include keyboard stands and custom storage for wiring.

Classrooms at the 700-student North Oldham Middle School in Goshen, Kentucky, feature operable walls to facilitate team teaching and large-group activities.

Children at Meridian Middle School in Buffalo Grove, Illinois, enjoy the upper-level commons area for independent reading, small-group activities and performances.

Classrooms at Williamsburg Middle/High School in Williamsburg, Ohio, are brightly lighted with room for a variety of seating arrangements.

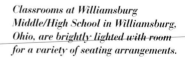

Teachers appreciate the ease with which they can view the media center from both levels at Meridian Middle School. Clear sightlines into the center enable teachers to monitor student activities and check on availability of computers and other resources. According to Principal Susan L. Mann, student temptation to disrupt media center activities from above has been minimal.

Located directly across from the main lobby in the academic realm of the building, the media center at Wilson Middle School in Muncie, Indiana, offers casual and small-group seating.

DEVELOPMENTALLY RESPONSIBLE MIDDLE LEVEL SCHOOLS ARE CHARACTERIZED BY:

- *Educators committed to young adolescents*

- *A shared vision*

- *High expectations for all*

- *An adult advocate for every student*

- *Family and community partnerships*

- *A positive school climate*

THEREFORE, DEVELOPMENTALLY RESPONSIVE MIDDLE LEVEL SCHOOLS PROVIDE:

- *Curriculum that is challenging, integrative, and exploratory*

- *Varied teaching and learning approaches*

- *Assessment and evaluation that promote learning*

- *Flexible organizational structures*

- *Programs and policies that foster health, wellness, and safety*

- *Comprehensive guidance and support services*

THE NATIONAL MIDDLE SCHOOL ASSOCIATION, *THIS WE BELIEVE*, 1995.

Rocks, Roller Coasters, And The Stock Market

"WE TRY TO TIE
SCIENCE INTO EVERYDAY
LIFE. THE STUDENTS
AREN'T ALL GOING TO
BECOME CHEMISTS AND
SCIENTISTS, BUT I WANT
THEM TO SEE HOW
SCIENCE RELATES TO
THE WORLD."

*—Louise Morello, Eighth-
Grade Science Teacher
and Department Chair,
Edgar Allan Poe Middle
School; Annandale, Virginia*

SCIENCE

M//T//W 10:10-11:00, F 10:10-11:55

MATH

M//T//W//TH 11:05-11:55

Stop into a science class at Angola Middle School in Angola, Indiana, and you might hear a discussion of how human bacteria has launched a multi-billion-dollar, international perfume and deodorant industry. At Edgar Allan Poe Middle School in Annandale, Virginia, eighth-graders in math and science may be checking the stock reports to review the latest figures for major consumer product and pharmaceutical companies. And at A.I. Root Middle School in Medina, Ohio, students may be exploring the density of a steamer

"We can get all 100 students on our team into the science room," says Penny Snyder, science teacher at Angola Middle School in Angola, Indiana. "That's the kind of space we need. I think it's wonderful to have room so that the kids can actually get up and move around and do hands-on activities."

trunk as a part of a unit reviewing the history of U.S. immigration, or analyzing data on roller coasters collected on a field trip to Cedar Point amusement park.

Around the country, science and math programs at the middle school level have evolved into creative yet practical initiatives that engage students through a combination of multimedia instruction, field experimentation, computer-based analysis, interactive research, and hands-on activities. Subject matter—as broad-ranging as analyzing the design of athletic shoes to predicting the weather—is often linked to curriculum in other academic areas, such as language arts, social studies, economics, and even physical education. "We try as much as possible to integrate the curriculum for our team," says Louise Morello, an eighth-grade science teacher and chair of the science department at Edgar Allan Poe Middle School. "I think it helps students understand the role that science plays, and how it affects their everyday lives."

While science curriculum in particular has become more inventive, the application of technology has also become routine. Rather than logging data by hand, for example, students use probeware linked to computers that automatically document and graph statistics such as temperature, light density, or pH levels. Computers, VCRs, laserdisk players, CD-ROMs, and innovative software programs supplement instruction and work well for both large and small groups. Many teachers use computers linked to large-screen monitors to demonstrate software or run multimedia presentations. "This is the way science is done today—on computers," says Morello. "We use computers for everything from data collection and experiments to tests. It's amazing how the students have come along with technology. And accessibility to computers is vital during class time—I use them all the time to reinforce a point or to answer questions. It's often spur-of-the-moment, which shows how integral the technology has become."

Students at Edgar Allan Poe Middle School in Annandale, Virginia, often use computers to assist in scientific experiments.

ROCKS, ROLLER COASTERS, AND THE STOCK MARKET

While computer-based instruction and creative curriculum keep students challenged, teachers are also focused on another important concern: safety. In science classes, glassware, hot plates, Bunsen burners, and chemicals present a host of potential hazards to students. Many teachers point to the classroom space itself as a factor in the safety of a science program. "I always worry about students getting cut or burned when the room is too crowded," says Morello, who moved into a more spacious classroom/lab when Poe Middle School was renovated and expanded. "Now, the room is big enough that students can spread out and work without bumping into each other or tripping. We can rearrange the tables several different ways. They can stand at the counters around the perimeter of the room, or work in small groups at the tables."

Tess Ewart, an eighth-grade teacher at A.I. Root Middle School in Medina, Ohio, agrees that space is critical to both safety and the quality of instruction in science. "It's great to have a larger room and more room to work," Ewart says. "We have space for the lab stations and for classroom instruction; and with the room layout, it's easy to watch and supervise—especially students working at the fume hood." Ewart points to the inclusion of a fume hood and eyewash station as important to the overall safety factor: "Having the fume hood and eyewash station has really made a difference in terms of safety. In our old

The science rooms at Wilson Middle School in Muncie, Indiana, include a fume hood, allowing students and staff to work with chemicals in a safe, well-ventilated area.

school, we didn't have proper ventilation—now I don't have to be concerned about the students inhaling vapors because of poor ventilation in the room."

Ewart and Morello also note that lockable storage is crucial within the science program. At Poe Middle

School, a large storeroom with a sink is shared by two science rooms. "We have a nice, large storeroom," says Morello. "About half of the space is used for teacher preparation, and the other half for chemical storage. We also have another chemical storage room down the hall, which is locked. Lockable storage is a big plus in the design—if the chemicals are too accessible you really have to keep an eye on everything."

At Angola Middle School, completion of the school's renovation and expansion meant new science labs in each of the grade-level wings. "We used to have four or five science classes going on at one time but only two labs," says seventh-grade science teacher Paul Beckwith. "It was like trying to go next door to cook at your neighbor's stove." A lack of running water and storage space for equipment and glassware also frustrated Angola Middle School teachers prior to the renovation. "We use more equipment and materials now than we did before," says sixth-grade science teacher Dean Harter. "It's convenient, and we can find things and do a lot more in the lab."

"Our new science rooms really support our program—in the past, our rooms were very small and limiting. The science program for this age group needs to be extremely interactive, and focused on problem-solving and trial and error. It's very hands-on."

—Hank Smith,
Superintendent
Celina City Schools, Ohio

"Having more sinks in the classroom is a big time-saver," says Poe Middle School science teacher Louise Morello. "We don't have to stop class several minutes early to start cleaning up, because there are more sinks to get the job done. It leaves us more instructional time."

Rocks, Roller Coasters, and the Stock Market

The outdoors is used extensively by students as part of A.I. Root Middle School's science program. Students have planted trees on Arbor Day, and recently studied rocks and crystals.

Many middle schools extend their science program into the outdoors. Use of environmental labs, gardens, ponds, wetland areas, forests, and fields enhances the study of wildlife, plants, rocks and minerals, the weather, and the environment in general. "We use the outdoors as often as we can," says William Nettles, a sixth-grade science teacher at A.I. Root Middle School. Sixth-grade projects have included mapping the woods by the school, a study of the nearby creek, rock identification, and making crystals.

"We built a weather station in the field next to our school," says Nettles. "It's equipped with thermometers, barometers, a wind vane, and a rain gauge. We've studied clouds and learned about forecasting the weather. The students really liked it, and we've been able to combine science, math, and writing—when we did our study of the weather, I asked the students to describe the weather each day. They were only allowed to use each adjective once a month, so once 'rainy' and 'cold' were used, it was a struggle. Toward the end of each month, we had a lot of creative ways to describe the weather."

"We have come as far as we can by changing schedules, organizing teachers and students into teams, and adding on to the already over-crowded curriculum. Now we must turn our attention to crafting the curriculum into what it must be: responsive to the unique and compelling needs of young adolescents."

—**Edward Brazee in Beyond Separate Subjects: Integrative Learning at the Middle Level** [1]

Sixth-grade students at A.I. Root Middle School in Medina, Ohio, studied the weather as a part of the school's earth science program. Named for an A.I. Root student, the Shawn Clark Weather Station houses barometers, thermometers, a wind vane, and a rain gauge.

[1] Siu-Runyan, Yvonne, and Faircloth, C. Victoria—Editors. *Beyond Separate Subjects: Integrative Learning at the Middle Level.* Christopher-Gordon Publishers, Inc., Northwood, MA, 1995. Page 21.

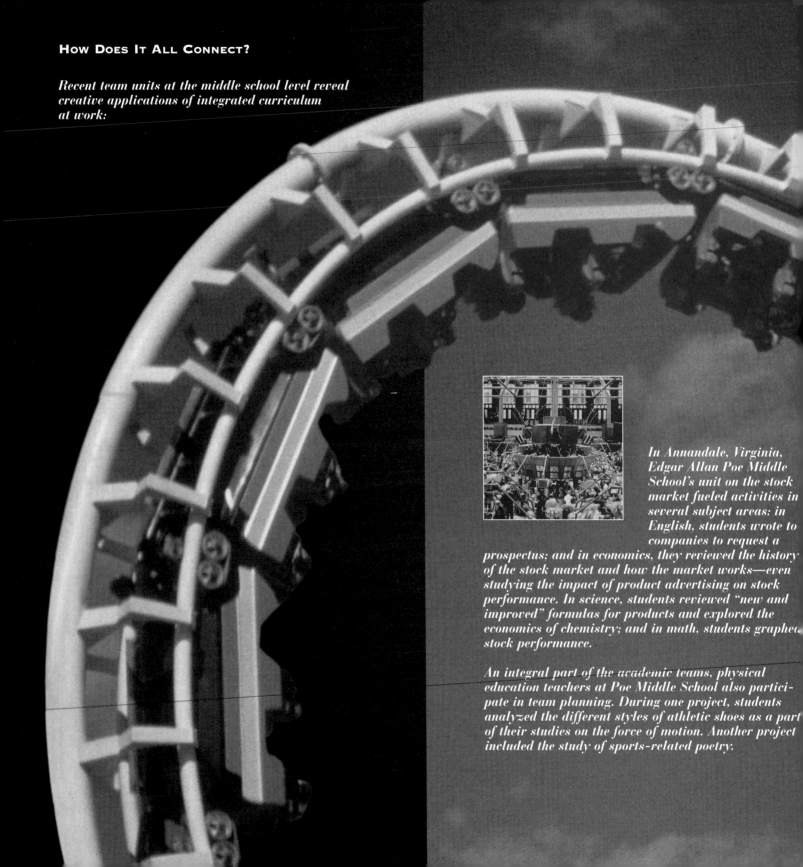

HOW DOES IT ALL CONNECT?

Recent team units at the middle school level reveal creative applications of integrated curriculum at work:

In Annandale, Virginia, Edgar Allan Poe Middle School's unit on the stock market fueled activities in several subject areas: in English, students wrote to companies to request a prospectus; and in economics, they reviewed the history of the stock market and how the market works—even studying the impact of product advertising on stock performance. In science, students reviewed "new and improved" formulas for products and explored the economics of chemistry; and in math, students graphed stock performance.

An integral part of the academic teams, physical education teachers at Poe Middle School also participate in team planning. During one project, students analyzed the different styles of athletic shoes as a part of their studies on the force of motion. Another project included the study of sports-related poetry.

In Medina, Ohio, A.I. Root Middle School's recent unit on roller coasters took two eighth-grade teams to Sandusky, Ohio, where they visited the historic Cedar Point amusement park. Studies ranged from mathematical and scientific data analysis of roller coasters to the history of Cedar Point, Lake Erie, and even the War of 1812.

The school's eighth-graders also recently studied immigration—reading novels and journals, learning songs, and studying films. In math and science, students examined the typical contents and volume of a steamer trunk and studied its density—including whether the trunk might sink or float during the sinking of a ship crossing to America.

A unit on "Walls" at Cooper Middle School in McLean, Virginia, explored famous walls such as the Berlin Wall and the Great Wall of China. Students also spent two days with professional architects simulating the construction of a wall for a cathedral, using gallon milk jugs filled with water and learning mathematical and structural engineering concepts such as load-bearing and non-load-bearing walls.

A sixth-grade unit on the Revolutionary War at Davey Middle School in Kent, Ohio, not only encompassed reading, history, and social studies assignments, it included a project in science on how to make pewter and studies of relative distances in math—such as the distance of Paul Revere's ride.

In Indianapolis, Indiana, Lincoln Middle School's unit on the Titanic embraced science and mathematical challenges as well as history and language arts. In a "Float Your Boat" unit, students designed ships using plastic soft drink bottles, and tested how much weight the "ships" could carry before sinking. In math, they constructed ships out of tag board and studied geometry using angles of the ships.

ANGOLA MIDDLE SCHOOL; ANGOLA, INDIANA

"When we started teaming here, all of the teachers were encouraged to design a class that we would really like to teach." says Scott Hottell, a seventh-grade language arts teacher. "I'm an avid outdoorsman, so I began teaching 'Adventure Literature.' All of the books we read get the kids to think about other places. I want to encourage them to travel and to create adventure in their lives—even in their own backyards."

The spirit of adventure that Hottell describes is not limited to his popular "Adventure Literature" class. Since the completion of Angola Middle School's comprehensive modernization, involving renovation of nearly 90,000 square feet of space and the addition of another 72,000 square feet, teachers have begun to incorporate more creative and ambitious projects into the curriculum, regularly working in collaboration with each other.

"We are offering courses that are just amazing for our kids," says Deborah Gilbert, an eighth-grade teacher in language arts, speech, and communications "I have a 'global communications' class that started out with writing and researching on the Internet. Now we're getting into Web design. I don't lecture at all. I give all of the instructions over e-mail. I never expected a class like this in my lifetime."

Glass walls at the rear of Angola Middle School's new media center overlook the school's playing fields and wooded site. A circular stair provides visual interest and access to a teacher resource room.

The Call Of the Wild
Jack London
WSP
WASHINGTON SQUARE PRESS

"ADVENTURE LITERATURE" READING LIST:

- *Moccasin Trail,* by Eloise Jarvis McGraw
- *Call Of The Wild* and *To Build A Fire,* by Jack London
- *Black Star, Bright Dawn,* by Scott O'Dell
- *I Heard The Owl Call My Name,* by Margaret Craven
- *Banner In The Sky,* by James Ramsey Ullman
- *Snowbound,* by Harry Mazer
- *Hatchet,* by Gary Paulsen
- *Treasure Island,* by Robert Louis Stevenson

"ADVENTURE LITERATURE"

Seventh-grade teacher Scott Hottell may be teaching language arts and literature, but his most popular course at Angola Middle School goes a long way toward whetting student appetites for the great outdoors. A class he developed in part because of his own interest in outdoor adventure, Hottell's "Adventure Literature" course covers both classic and contemporary fiction that explores subjects ranging from pirates to mountain climbing.

"Survival is a common theme in many of these books," says Hottell. "I encourage the students to think about survival in extreme situations, and using their minds to overcome the challenges." His reading list represents a cross-section of cultures and historical timeframes; and he ties in the literature discussion with Internet research—often enabling students to go back in time and then return to the present moment, as in a recent study of the Iditerod. "We read Scott O'Dell's Black Star, Bright Dawn," *says Hottell, "which is about the Iditerod race in Alaska. We read it during March, when the Iditerod starts. We studied the history of the race, and using the Internet, we were able to track the race itself on a daily basis. We even got the Iditerod rules—all 25 pages of them—from the Internet, and the students learned those as well."*

Angola Middle School; Angola, Indiana

Modernization of Angola Middle School created grade-level clusters to facilitate teaming. "We're more cohesive in a lot of the things we do," says Penny Snyder, a science teacher. "Before, we didn't have a chance to interact with each other even if we had the same students. I think we've provided more balance for the students. For example, if someone's giving a test on one day, we all know about it—so we don't all give tests and overwhelm them." Hottell agrees that teaming has its advantages: "With teaming, there is a lot of mutual support and interactive planning. And if you have a wacky idea, you have several people all saying they will help you."

While teaming does enable teachers to moderate student workload, eighth-grade teachers at Angola Middle School conspire to push their students as much as possible every Wednesday afternoon—during "Brain Bowl." Held in the new large-group instruction room, Brain Bowl features two teams of students, competing in a quiz show format—complete with an automatic timer, lights, and buzzers. "We purchased machinery that allows students to buzz in when

Classrooms at Angola Middle School are large enough to permit flexible seating arrangements. Sloped projection walls aid in multimedia presentations.

A greenhouse was added to Angola Middle School during its renovation, allowing students to study plant life and plant care, photosynthesis, and hydroponics. Teachers also take advantage of the woods and wetlands area behind the school: "Our students have logged 52 species of plant life on our site," says Principal William Church.

ANGOLA MIDDLE SCHOOL; ANGOLA, INDIANA

they have the answer," says William Church, the school's principal. "All of the questions are developed from that week's studies. It's very student-driven, and the kids have a lot of fun with it."

"Kids at this age level work better when they have a chance to get up and move around," says language arts teacher Joe Kennedy about the large-group instruction room. "You can really move around in there—split the students up into small groups and give them a little more freedom. Their brains seem to work quicker when we let them get up on their feet."

"The large-group instruction room is one of the results of teachers being involved in the planning of this renovation," says science teacher Gary Kearney. "That room is used all the time—it's the heart of the building."

Angola Middle School's new computer lab provides instructional space for students, as well as for teacher training.

"During construction, there was a big plywood wall near the media center," says science teacher Gary Kearney. *"We had the students paint a 'Wall of Respect.' The kids could design a section and put up something about anyone they respected or loved, or who had affected their lives. Everybody here read it, and I don't think anybody walked away without a tear in their eye."*

I WANT TO DEDICATE MY peice OF THE WALL to the constrUction workers Who Gave us the wall and who are Makins the school look better and makins it Better

CHALLENGE

MARCH MADNESS

Choose an animal that is also a team mascot—such as the Ball State Cardinals or the Penn State Nittany Lions. Describe your animal. What does it look like? Where does it usually live? What does it eat? Why do you think it was chosen as a mascot? Draw a picture, and prepare a three-minute presentation for the class.

—AN ASSIGNMENT FROM "MARCH MADNESS," A THEME UNIT USED AT ANGOLA MIDDLE SCHOOL IN ANGOLA, INDIANA.

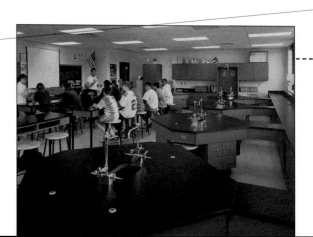

Science rooms at Lincoln Middle School in Indianapolis, Indiana, incorporate computers on ledges—above the lab stations and away from sinks.

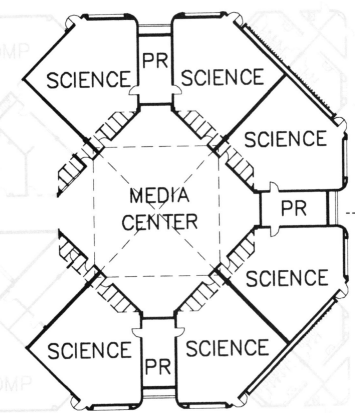

During a recent expansion, Reynoldsburg Junior High School in Reynoldsburg, Ohio, gained new science facilities. Operable walls enable classes to work as a large group. Each room features multiple sinks and built-in cabinetry.

The science labs at the new Crestview Middle School in Huntington, Indiana, are clustered around the media center at the core of the academic wing. Two science classrooms are positioned directly across the hall from each of the grade-level pods, enabling the science program to work as part of the team units. Grouping the rooms at the academic core also allows the program to work as a department. Proximity to the media center—which features a large skylight—also enables the science rooms to take advantage of the natural light.

Colorful cabinetry and perimeter lab stations highlight the spacious science rooms at Woodridge Middle School in Peninsula, Ohio.

At Hamilton Southeastern Junior High School in Fishers, Indiana, ample natural daylight supports instruction in plant life.

Time To Eat, Shop, and Play

LUNCH
12:00-12:45

Students at Meridian Middle School in Buffalo Grove, Illinois, have a special reason to appreciate their lunch break: they were instrumental in choosing their own food service vendor. Several fifth-graders recently took part in a comprehensive research project in which they surveyed other schools about their food service programs, then—using classroom telephones—contacted vendors about services and menu options. When it came time to negotiate, the students took part in the process and helped make the final selection.

The cafeteria at Meridian Middle School in Buffalo Grove, Illinois, has an operable wall (right) that opens into the gym for large assemblies.

Though most middle school students don't have an opportunity to review menus and negotiate contracts, they typically do agree that lunch is one of the most important times of the day. A chance to eat, relax, and chat with friends provides a needed break from a demanding schedule. Some students use the time to stop at their lockers, catch up on homework, visit the school supply store, and participate in tutoring or interest-based clubs. Many schools also offer a "recess," including games and active indoor/outdoor play, during the lunch period.

"Before we transitioned from a junior high school to a middle school, we didn't have a 'recess' break," says Tom McKenna, principal of A.I. Root Middle School in Medina, Ohio. "We were bringing in sixth-graders at that point, and it seemed like a good opportunity to add in that kind of a break for all of the students. Our lunch period now is a combination of lunch and recess. We have a big trunk in the cafetorium with table games and electronic games, we have ping pong and foosball up on the stage, and the students can go outside."

McKenna, who also has an elementary school background, believes that recess is instrumental in giving students at the middle school level an informal break in their day. "It's a legitimate part of their day," says McKenna. "I believe that the students do better academically when recess is a part of the program. In a way, everybody needs it—even adults." The school also has a jukebox in the cafetorium, which students are permitted to play during lunch. "It actually helps us keep noise under control," says McKenna. "When the noise level gets too high in the cafetorium, we just turn down the jukebox. The students have to quiet down to hear the music." McKenna adds that, at 25 cents a song, the jukebox is an "invisible fundraiser—we use the profits for student recognition and awards programs."

"It seems as if it takes the average middle school kid about six minutes to eat lunch. They need other activities so that they don't get into trouble. We have intramurals in the gym and on the playing fields and a brown bag book club in the library."

—Dr. Marc Crail,
Superintendent, Kent City
Schools, Ohio

Time To Eat, Shop, And Play

While the lunch period is a favorite with many students, others may find this time of day to be intimidating or frustrating—especially for new students. Walking into a large cafeteria with long rows of tables and unfamiliar faces can be unnerving for shy students, and may even cause them to avoid eating altogether. Long food service lines or congested serving areas may also cause the lunch break to lose appeal.

Well-designed and furnished cafeteria space minimizes these concerns, and helps create a more pleasant and orderly environment. A variety of table arrangements, including round and rectangular configurations, enables students to sit in smaller clusters and avoids the "institutional" look of rows of long tables. Some cafeterias at the middle school level also offer booth seating and smaller areas for groups of two or three. Many administrators find that allowing students to sit in smaller groups makes supervision easier and helps with noise control.

The auditeria at Avondale Middle School in Rochester Hills, Michigan, features a tiered floor and a raised stage with acoustical panels and multi-level lighting system control.

Ample natural daylight, acoustical treatment, and durable furnishings and floor treatment are imperative to a successful dining environment. As the space often serves many purposes—including assemblies and performances—many schools opt to include a stage adjacent to the dining space. A *cafetorium* typically features a stage at one end of the room, portable seating and adjacent storage that permit a variety of configurations, enhanced acoustical treatment, and a single-level floor. An *auditeria* also includes a stage and portable seating, but often has a tiered floor and may offer more sophisticated acoustical treatment and advanced lighting and sound systems.

The cafetorium at North Oldham Middle School in Goshen, Kentucky, offers booth seating. Students also enjoy board games such as chess and checkers during their lunch breaks.

Regardless of whether a middle school incorporates a traditional cafeteria, a cafetorium, or an auditeria, versatility and size are important considerations: "We get a tremendous amount of use out of our new auditeria," says Virgil Taueg, principal of Lincoln Middle School in Indianapolis, Indiana. "On a daily basis, the space is used for many activities—but since this school opened, we've also been able to do a lot of special functions that we could never have done before. On Grandparents' Day, we had 600 kids and over 175 guests. If we had tried to do it before, in our old cafeteria, those grandparents would have had to sit on top of the tables because there wasn't enough room! And on the same day, when the grandparents left after lunch, we cleared the auditeria and had it set for a school board meeting that evening. It was entirely transformed."

A.I. ROOT MIDDLE SCHOOL; MEDINA, OHIO

A.I. Root Middle School Principal Tom McKenna believes that first impressions count: "When a person walks into a school—a student, parent, or someone from the community—you only have about 30 seconds to make them feel welcome. It's especially important for new students—the impression we make with this building can help reduce their stress and make them feel at home."

A strong advocate of enlivening the school building with student displays, special exhibits, posters, artwork, and banners, McKenna's philosophy of creating a welcoming environment is also reflected in the building design itself. He and several other administrators and faculty members participated in the planning process for the 700-student school, which is set in the heart of a new

residential community. The building features a landscaped plaza and walkways at the front of the school and a main office with large windows to create an open—rather than intimidating—effect.

Hallways near the main entry are filled with natural daylight and are lively reminders of A.I. Root's pervasive

The public wing of the building (at left) includes separate entrances for the community and can be secured from the academic areas. The school's stage opens to both the cafetorium and the gym. In the academic zone of the building, the media center is centrally located to each of the three grade-level pods.

Set in the midst of a growing suburban neighborhood, A. I. Root Middle School's 40-acre wooded site is frequently used for nature experiments and outdoor studies. A landscaped plaza at the school's front entry welcomes students and the community.

school spirit and pride—as well as its student-centered approach to learning. Display cases and exhibits—including a large mural—showcase artwork and assignments and highlight student achievements. "Displaying student work throughout the school gives our kids a chance to feel ownership in this building," says McKenna. "We see the results in reduced vandalism, and the way they take care of the property."

Another objective that emerged early-on in the planning process was the desire to keep noisier activities—such as band, orchestra, physical education, and dining—clustered together in the public wing of the building, apart from academic areas. Lunch-time in particular provides a lively break for students, who use the stage for ping pong and foosball games, and play games such as checkers and chess at their tables. The

stage is positioned between the gym and the cafetorium, with operable walls that allow the stage to be opened to either space.

"Our stage is in use all day long," says Assistant Principal Mike Pallini. "The orchestra class uses it every morning for three periods, then we clear it for lunch and 'indoor recess.' With the operable walls, we can open the stage to the gym and have concerts. It gives us flexibility and saves us a lot of time."

Students at A.I. Root enjoy a variety of activities at lunchtime, including games at their tables and up on the stage. "The games have worked out very well," says Principal Tom McKenna. "The students are very good about waiting their turn to play."

Team planning is facilitated by the inclusion of centralized teacher workrooms in each of the pods at A.I. Root Middle School.

School spirit and pride are evident throughout the building, where hallways showcase student artwork and achievements.

"I think our school store is a really good idea because we can get a lot of supplies that we need. There are pens and scissors, crayons—anything that you have run out of and need to replace."

—Brittany Sarmas, Fifth-Grade Student, Meridian Middle School, Buffalo Grove, Illinois

The auditeria at South Vermillion Middle School offers round and rectangular seating. Adjustable tables provide aided comfort for middle school students, regardless of height.

Students at South Vermillion Middle School in Clinton, Indiana, have a chance to visit the school's book and supply store during their lunch period.

In Muncie, Indiana, Wilson Middle School's food service program uses a "scatter" approach that enables students to choose from a variety of food stations, including a salad bar.

The cafeteria at Wilson Middle School also serves as a lobby and commons/surge space for the school's auditorium, natatorium, and two gymnasiums.

A POSITIVE SCHOOL CLIMATE

The climate of a developmentally responsive middle level school is safe, inviting, and caring; it promotes a sense of community and encourages learning. A visitor walking into a middle level building immediately develops some first impressions. The cordial, pleasant tone of the staff and the way students greet and treat each other are revealing. Interactions among staff members and between students and staff reflect democracy and fairness. In a healthy school environment, human relationships are paramount, and all individuals are treated with dignity and respect. Students and adults recognize and accept one another's differences; curiosity, creativity, and diversity are celebrated.

THE NATIONAL MIDDLE SCHOOL ASSOCIATION,
THIS WE BELIEVE, 1995.

Time To Eat, Shop, And Play

The cafeteria at Discovery Middle School in Granger, Indiana, is a brightly lighted area with a variety of seating options. Long rows of tables can also be divided into smaller rectangular seating.

The cafeteria at Thomas A. Edison Middle School in South Bend, Indiana, enjoys views into a landscaped courtyard.

The cafeteria at Central Junior High School in West Melbourne, Florida, features a stage that also opens to the school's courtyard for open-air performances. Students often take their lunches outdoors as well.

The food service area at
Central Junior High School
offers students a variety of
a la carte and snack options.

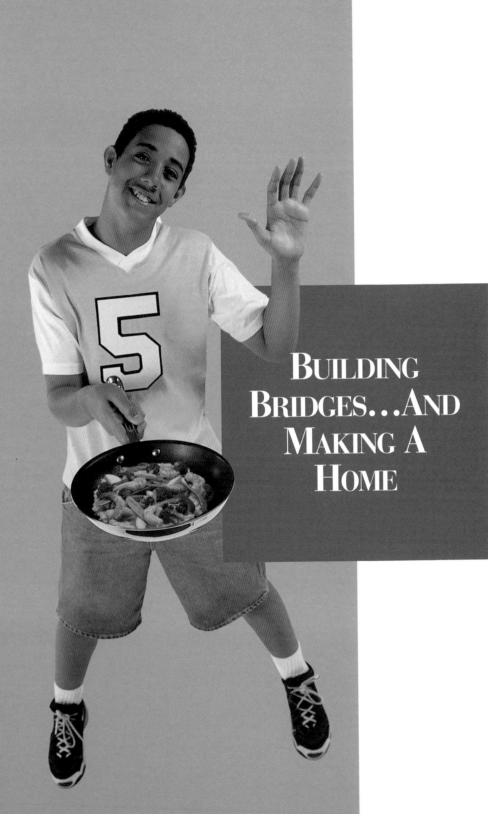

BUILDING BRIDGES...AND MAKING A HOME

"AT THE MIDDLE SCHOOL LEVEL IN PARTICULAR, WE NEED TO CAPITALIZE ON THE STUDENTS' INNATE CURIOSITY AND ENERGY LEVEL—WE NEED TO GIVE THEM A VARIETY OF OPPORTUNITIES TO EXPLORE."

—Dr. David E. Sawyer,
Superintendent,
School Board of Brevard
County, Florida

**APPLIED TECHNOLOGY
M/W/F 12:50-1:40
HOME ECONOMICS/FASHION LAB
T/TH 12:50-1:40**

"My role as a teacher has always been to motivate and educate," says Tom Milam, industrial technology teacher at South Vermillion Middle School in Clinton, Indiana. "Now, our new lab—with all of its technology—provides a lot of that motivation. The students love it, and their energy level has been unreal. It's changed my role—I spend less time motivating and more time educating."

Many of the computers in the industrial technology lab at South Vermillion Middle School in Clinton, Indiana, are linked to machinery and tools. Students turn on a light above their modules if they need extra help from their teacher, who is able to facilitate and work one-on-one as needed.

The opening of the new South Vermillion Middle School, which replaced a long-outdated building, provided an ideal opportunity for a transition from a traditional industrial arts curriculum to a modern, applied technology program—a crucial change according to Milam. Like many school districts around the country, the South Vermillion Community School Corporation has incorporated a modular approach to its technology program—allowing students to participate in a variety of hands-on tasks, such as operating a computer-controlled lathe; analyzing and building a small engine; building and operating a robot; using a wind tunnel; building model rockets; and studying aerodynamics, energy, power, transportation, and structural technology.

Rolland Voris, a technology instructor at Lincoln Middle School in Indianapolis, Indiana, offers a similar assessment of his school's program: "Our industrial arts program has really evolved over the past few years," he says. "The computer-driven, modular lab approach to instruction has really come into its own. It's an interactive approach, capturing instruction, reading material, assignments, testing, and evaluation. As a delivery system, the modular approach actually gives us much better class-room management and accountability. It saves instructional time on a day-to-day basis, and allows us to facilitate more—it gives us more time to plan and manage the students' work.

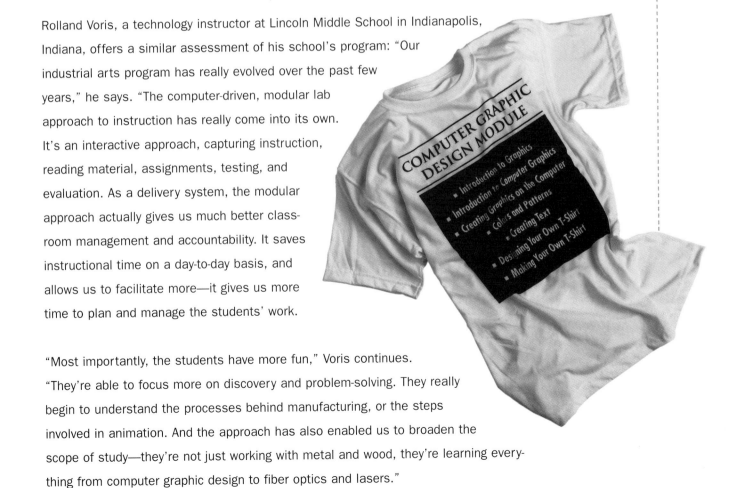

"Most importantly, the students have more fun," Voris continues. "They're able to focus more on discovery and problem-solving. They really begin to understand the processes behind manufacturing, or the steps involved in animation. And the approach has also enabled us to broaden the scope of study—they're not just working with metal and wood, they're learning everything from computer graphic design to fiber optics and lasers."

A number of workplace skills, such as communication and teamwork, are also integral to applied technology programs at the middle school level. "Students need to be able to read technical manuals, write reports, work at a keyboard, and get along with other students—just as they will when they are employees," says Dr. David E. Sawyer, superintendent of the School Board of Brevard County, Florida. "It's impossible to prepare them for all the specific skills that they may need, because today many of those skills are unique to each employer. We want the students to have basic occupational skills and an understanding of decision-making processes that are relevant to the workplace.

A suite of classrooms featuring automated, modular instructional units serves the applied technology and home economics programs at Discovery Middle School in Granger, Indiana. Students entering the classrooms determine the day's assignment by checking electronic message boards—another time-saver for the teachers.

"We focus on the 'Three R's,'" says Dr. Sawyer. "First, the curriculum in applied technology should be relevant. It should be practical in terms of the students' day-to-day lives. The studies should also be realistic—they shouldn't be make-believe. Naturally, we want the students using keyboards, not manual typewriters; and microwave ovens instead of coal-burning stoves—but this applies to all of the technology program. It's why, for example, we're seeing more industrial technology programs—with lasers, biotechnology, and robotics—instead of an emphasis on traditional woodworking. The new curriculum is still hands-on—students manipulate, construct, and analyze—but it has more practical applications for today. Third, we want the technology program to be rewarding," Dr. Sawyer continues. "We want the students to appreciate and value what they're learning, and to enhance their abilities to achieve their aspirations."

Is there still a role for the traditional shop activities—with hammers, saws, and drill presses? Most administrators and teachers agree that there is a need for this aspect, but the focus—and facilities required to house these activities—have been minimized in many schools. "Fabrication is still important," says Dr. Sawyer, "because it gives students the opportunity to work with raw material through to the finished product. Overall, however, we've moved to a much more technological program."

Tom Alexander, principal at the new Crestview Middle School in Huntington, Indiana, agrees. Within the school's "Related Arts" program—encompassing industrial technology, computer education, home economics, art, band and choir, physical education, fitness, and wellness—the industrial technology program in particular has been transformed over the past few years. "Most of our program in industrial technology is computer-driven," he says. "As a result, it's very student-centered. But I am a traditionalist in some respects—I still think kids ought to be able to do a little cooking, mending, and sewing when they leave here; and we have a small workshop with tools."

Students participate in self-directed, modular instructional units as a part of Central Junior High School's applied technology curriculum in West Melbourne, Florida.

"When we whip egg whites for waffles, we're talking about physics, and how the egg batter will make the waffles rise," says Lois Hall, a work and family studies instructor at Edgar Allan Poe Middle School in Annandale, Virginia. "When we design and sew beach bags, we're using math concepts—studying dimensions, perimeters, and angles. We're constantly teaching math and science here, but more importantly, we're teaching life skills—not just how to cook and sew, but how to plan, prepare, document, and follow through. The students work independently and in small groups—just as we do as adults in the working world."

Although in many respects home economics and consumer science courses have not evolved as rapidly as other applied technology programs, they are often centered around an integrated curriculum approach that helps to build practical, lifelong skills for students. "We really focus on decision-making skills and working together as a team," says Debbie Bock, family consumer science teacher at A.I. Root Middle School in

BUILDING BRIDGES...AND MAKING A HOME

Medina, Ohio. "When the students go on to their careers, they will be working as teams—whether in businesses or factories. They also learn a lot here about time management."

Bock, who has been teaching for 26 years, participated in the planning of A.I. Root Middle School, which gave her an opportunity to help design the home economics space. "We divided the space into a carpeted classroom area and a kitchen with a tile floor," says Bock. "The classroom area is large and flexible, so that we're able to use it for tests, lectures, overhead presentations, or working in small groups. I also asked for a separate space for a laundry area, which has been a big help. Because it's separate from the classroom, it doesn't disrupt the class. Other teachers can access it if they need to without interrupting my class. It's also a good storage area."

In addition to learning broad-based time management and decision-making skills, the students in Bock's class learn many practical, hands-on skills—in nutrition and cooking, child care, and sewing and crafts. "The students enjoy the simple hand sewing projects,"

Teacher Debbie Bock helped to design the home economics classroom at A. I. Root Middle School in Medina, Ohio. She opted for a combination of classroom and kitchen space, with a partial wall dividing the areas. The room also features a separate laundry and storage area.

The home economics classroom at Hamilton Southeastern Junior High School in Fishers, Indiana, features both tiled and carpeted classroom areas. Large mirrors suspended from the ceiling facilitate student viewing of cooking demonstrations.

says Bock. "It gives them a sense of accomplishment. I had one student who went home and took all of his boy scout badges off of his uniform and then sewed them back on—he wanted to do it exactly the way I had taught him."

Lois Hall says that she sees an "immense difference" in her program since the completion of Poe Middle School's recent modernization and expansion. "We had a much smaller area before," she says, "and it was very awkward for a large class. Now we're able to have classroom instruction and lab activities at the same time. The space is also light and airy now—before it was depressing. I really want them to develop a lot of skills and this space is designed to allow a number of hands-on activities.

"The most important thing that I see come out of this class is the development of their self-confidence," Hall points out. "With some projects, students will say, 'I don't think I can do that'—but they can and it really helps their confidence."

EDGAR ALLAN POE MIDDLE SCHOOL; ANNANDALE, VIRGINIA

According to teachers and administrators, enhanced communications and teaming opportunities are direct results of the modernization and expansion of Edgar Allan Poe Middle School in Annandale, Virginia. "Because of the way this school is designed now, our teachers are closer and can communicate better," says Principal June C. Monterio. "I've seen powerful outcomes that result from the informal dynamics that this space allows—teachers are able to say, 'Look at what I'm working on,' and interact across grade levels, across disciplines, at every level."

Poe Middle School was reconfigured from a seventh- and eighth-grade building to a 1,200-student school with grades six through eight.

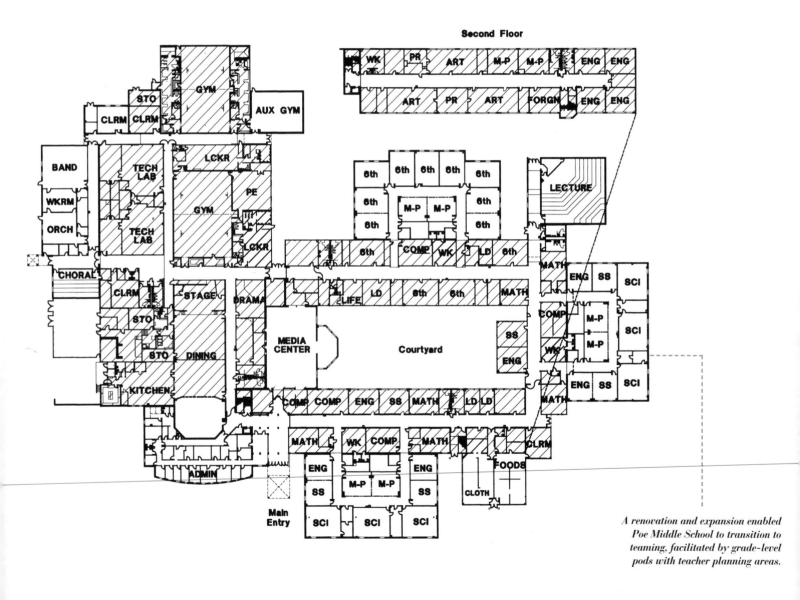

A renovation and expansion enabled Poe Middle School to transition to teaming, facilitated by grade-level pods with teacher planning areas.

The new lecture hall at Poe Middle School is in constant use by classes, as well as administration meetings system-wide. "We use it for skits and dramatic readings," says English teacher Natasha Heny. "It's important for the students to learn to feel comfortable in front of an audience."

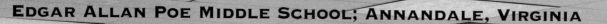

The modernization included the addition of an auxiliary gymnasium; a music suite; a new media center; a tiered lecture hall; administrative space; and several classrooms, labs, multi-purpose rooms, and support areas. The entire existing building was also renovated.

"The way this school has been renovated makes it a lot easier on teachers," says James Shepherd, a seventh-grade math and science teacher. "We have more flexibility in working with the students, and supervision is much easier." Sheila Chenard, an eighth-grade math teacher, also points out that, "The brightness of this building really affects you. We're much more upbeat and so are the students."

A classroom with a raised platform provides a suitable venue for meetings, presentations, skits, and small awards programs and ceremonies.

Multi-purpose rooms with operable walls add to the flexibility of each grade-level pod.

The renovation and expansion of Poe Middle School yielded a larger, more flexible media center: "The library is excellent now," says Betsy Lockman, a sixth-grade language arts and science teacher. "Two or three classes can use it at the same time."

Expanded facilities at Poe Middle School accommodate both an applied technology program utilizing a modular delivery system, and a traditional shop area—enabling students to take fabrication projects, such as the construction of candy machines, from start to finish.

Natasha Heny, an eighth-grade English teacher, appreciates the bright and spacious classrooms that resulted from the modernization: "It's so important to have a comfortable, flexible environment—especially for middle school students,"

she says. "They're having a tough time controlling their bodies and their emotions—so the more you can control the environment the better. You need to be able to change the lighting, or the arrangement of the room."

Monterio also credits the design of the

building with making it easier to include and support children with special needs, such as those in the ESL and LD programs: "The pods give them built-in support because they are in constant contact with their team of teachers, who all know them."

"We constantly apply academic subjects to our work," says Lois Hall, a work and family studies teacher at Poe Middle School, "especially math and science." Coursework in sewing—which requires creating custom patterns—has included making beach bags and boxer shorts.

CHALLENGE

"MAKING THE FAMILY MEAL"

Students are to plan, prepare, and clean up the kitchen after the chosen meal. Parents, please monitor the plans of your child to ensure that your family's budget, your child's skill level, time constraints, and your personal considerations are respected.

The meal may be breakfast, lunch, or dinner. It may be simple and inexpensive or complicated and expensive without impacting his/her grade. What is important is that there will be new learning for the student. The report (handwritten or word-processed) will include the following:

- *Menu—written in correct menu format, with recipes of food prepared*

- *Work plan—planned sequence of activities; remember table setting and clean-up*

- *Narrative—student-written summary and evaluation of work completed. This may include visuals such as drawings and snapshots.*

- *Comments and signatures—of family and/or friends who ate the meal*

- *Optional: cost analysis—calculate the cost per serving*

—FAMILY MEAL ASSIGNMENT FROM EDGAR ALLAN POE MIDDLE SCHOOL'S "TEEN LIVING" COURSE—PART OF THE WORK AND FAMILY STUDIES PROGRAM TAUGHT BY LOIS HALL

TEEN LIVING MEAL ASSIGNMENT

MENU

Chili Over Pasta
Corn
Texas Garlic Toast
Orange Cranberry Fruit Punch
Bananas And Crushed Oreos Over Frozen Yogurt

RECIPE

1 package of ground beef (16 oz)
kidney beans (15 oz)
canned chunky tomatoes (14 1/2 oz)
1/2 package San Giorgio Pasta (8 oz)
Contadina Tomato Sauce (8 oz)
McCormick Chili Powder (1.25 oz)
olive oil (1 teaspoon)
Sargento Shredded Cheese (as much as desired)
sour cream (as much as desired)

BEVERAGE

Twister Orange Cranberry Fruit
Punch (12 oz)

SIDE DISHES

1 package Texas Toast (11.25 oz)
corn (11 oz)

DESSERT

frozen yogurt (1 pint)
1 banana
crushed Oreo Cookies (as much as desired)

WORK PLAN

PREPARATION

6:00 - wash hands
6:02 - get out all cooking equipment and ingredients
6:07 - heat olive oil in large skillet
6:09 - add meat and stir until brown
6:19 - wash and open tops of cans, continue stirring meat
6:24 - add and stir in all cans to meat
6:25 - turn heat down to low, let chili simmer
6:27 - fill large sauce pan 2/3 up with water, heat on high until boiling point
6:30 - while waiting for water to boil rinse out cans
6:33 - preheat oven at 425 degrees for Texas Toast
6:35 - set timer for 7 minutes
6:38 - open can of corn and dump into sauce pan, heat on high
6:40 - wrap cookie sheet in aluminum foil
6:42 - take pasta off burner and pour into strainer
6:44 - place Texas Toast on cookie sheet and put in oven
6:45 - turn heat down on corn, let simmer
6:49 - flip toast in oven
6:50 - begin setting table (put plates and cups on table, wrap fork and knife in napkin, light candles)

6:52 - take toast out of oven and put in bread basket
6:53 - finish setting table
6:55 - make juice (pour frozen concentrate into pitcher and add 3 cups of water, stir)

6:58 - **EAT**

CLEAN-UP

7:25 - begin clean-up (clear table, blow out candles, wipe table and counter, put away any ingredients, wash dishes)

8:00 - finish with clean up

DESSERT

9:00 - scoop frozen yogurt into bowl
9:03 - slice banana onto yogurt
9:05 - crush oreos and add to yogurt
9:07 - indulge!
9:08 - clean up (put away oreos, trash, wash plates)
9:11 - REMEMBER TO EAT OUT TOM

When teacher Lois Hall asked students to prepare a family meal at home as an assignment in their Teen Living course, she had no idea just how creative and thorough they could be. Menus ranged from "veggie pizza" and homemade brownies to Insalata di Caprese, garlic papaya shrimp, and Key Lime pie. The students planned their menus, did the shopping, set the table, prepared the meal, and cleaned up. They also enjoyed a hard-earned family meal, and began to appreciate the work that goes into feeding a family.

For one student—seventh-grader Andrew Satten—the experience was an "eye opener" according to his report, which earned an "A." At times, he felt as if he were "stirring forever," and noted that "cleaning up took a long time—especially washing the dishes." Now an expert at chili over pasta and "Texas garlic toast," Andrew concluded that, "Next time I make a meal I'll try to clean up as I go along so I don't have one big clean-up at the end. I definitely learned a great deal from this project and hopefully I'll be able to incorporate these new skills I picked up into future meals I make."

Andrew's conclusions were exactly as Lois Hall had hoped for all of her students. "I wanted them to apply the skills they've learned here in class," she says. "The project covered everything from analyzing the costs per serving to lighting candles and folding napkins. Their documentation and reports were very impressive, and they were imaginative with their menus. But I knew that this was successful when all the kids came back saying, 'I don't know how my parents do this night after night!'"

Poe Middle School's "Family Meal" Assignment

"This experience was certainly an eye opener. I had no idea how much work was put into making a simple meal."

—ANDREW SATTEN, SEVENTH-GRADE STUDENT, EDGAR ALLAN POE MIDDLE SCHOOL; ANNANDALE, VIRGINIA

PIKE TOWNSHIP TECHNOLOGY EDUCATION

"The first goal of the Pike Township Technology Education Curriculum will be to begin developing technological literacy. The middle school students will start developing technological skills necessary for communication, creative thinking, and decision-making, as well as the ability to apply these skills to solve technical problems. As an integral part of the program, students will explore career opportunities and study relationships and applications of math, science, and communications skills to our technological world.

Technology Education, a related arts class, is an exciting, challenging, activity-centered subject area for students with every kind of interest and career goal. Technology Education is the use of knowledge, tools, and skills to solve practical problems and to extend our human capabilities. The technology students need to be exposed to the activities that best illustrate the present application of technical materials by conducting experiments, using computers to design/solve a variety of technological problems, testing solutions, producing documents, gaining better understanding of the value of energy; and initiating better understanding about the use of resources and information. Technology students will be directly involved with learning as they develop a better understanding of our increasingly complex society."

—FROM THE EDUCATIONAL SPECIFICATIONS FOR THE NEW LINCOLN MIDDLE SCHOOL IN INDIANAPOLIS, INDIANA. STUDENTS AT LINCOLN STUDY A BROAD RANGE OF TECHNOLOGY AREAS—FROM COMPUTER SOFTWARE APPLICATION AND DESKTOP PUBLISHING TO FLIGHT SIMULATION AND ROBOTICS.

All of the computers in Lincoln Middle School's technology classroom are networked. Students manage their own coursework as they rotate through the various units, studying such subjects as "Exploratory Electronics" and "Fluid Power."

The technology lab at A.I. Root Middle School in Medina, Ohio, features both traditional machinery and computer modules.

Students at Lincoln Middle School in Indianapolis, Indiana, participate in a range of hands-on activities, including cooking projects and setting a table.

Hamilton Southeastern Junior High School in Fishers, Indiana, offers students both a traditional shop experience and automated instruction in its duplex of spacious applied technology classrooms.

LESSONS FOR LIFE

HEALTH AND PHYSICAL EDUCATION
M//W//F 1:45-3:00

Take a quick look at physical education programs in middle schools today, and it may not seem as if much has changed over the years. The curriculum still focuses on the basics of health and fitness: aerobic exercise, individual and team sports, strength training, rhythm and dance, recreational activities, nutrition, and personal hygiene. An emphasis on the importance of physical fitness—lessons for life—continues to be an integral part of middle school education.

Take a closer look at these programs, however, and some crucial changes in P.E. instruction become apparent. First, the delivery of instruction has evolved: teachers are tapping into more creative opportunities to introduce fun sports and recreational activities that can be enjoyed throughout life, such as in-line skating, golf, tennis, and aerobic dance. Informal competitions, such as school-based "Olympic" challenges in a variety of sports, also help build enthusiasm and individual and team commitment. Many of these tournaments and events are organized and managed by the students themselves, as an added measure of engaging children in the overall competition.

Technological resources have enhanced the scope of P.E. instruction, including heart monitors, computer-based instruction programs, Internet research sites, and multimedia presentation tools. Instructors are also broadening fitness programs to include a greater emphasis on classroom-based learning, enabling students to focus more readily on health and nutrition issues, substance abuse, disease prevention, anatomy, and mental health.

Facilities housing physical education activities have evolved as well—in part to accommodate program changes. If financially feasible, many schools at the middle school level opt for both a spectator gym and an auxiliary or "practice" gym, which helps to accommodate expanded schedules for team and tournament sport use, intramurals, practices, and community use. Girls' sports in particular have benefited from increased access to gymnasium facilities, and the operation of two gyms simplifies daily P.E. scheduling—especially during inclement weather when outdoor fields and structures can't be used.

Facilities for P.E. now routinely incorporate classrooms near gymnasiums and weight rooms. "The classrooms are really important for pulling students in for a lesson on how the cardiovascular system works, for example, or studies in nutrition and health," says Sheila Toth, a physical fitness instructor at Discovery Middle School in Granger, Indiana. "When they are all sitting on the gym floor, it's hard to get them into that mode of learning—it's difficult for them to focus and take notes. When they're in the gym, they really want to play."

"Having the health classrooms near our gym area has really helped our program and saved us a lot of time," says Jayne Bennett, a physical education and health teacher at Edgar Allan Poe Middle School in Annandale, Virginia. During a recent modernization, the P.E. area at Poe Middle School was renovated and expanded, which included adding an

The North Oldham Middle School Mustangs play before a home crowd in their new 9,200-square-foot gymnasium in Goshen, Kentucky.

"I like the auxiliary gym we have now. It's nice to have a separate gym where we can practice at night and everything is not so crammed. And the girls can practice, and practices aren't so late at night because there are two gyms."

—Leah Seevers, Eighth-Grade Student, Angola Middle School; Angola, Indiana

auxiliary gym and two classrooms for health instruction. "The permanent health rooms have enabled us to bring in more resources and exhibits," Bennett says. "We no longer have to lug materials around to different classrooms to try to teach health. It really confirms that health instruction is not just an afterthought, but a vital part of the curriculum."

Perhaps the most important change in P.E. instruction in recent years is that the message itself—*take care of your health*—has become significantly more urgent. "We're raising a generation of unhealthy children," says Bennett, who has been teaching P.E. for nearly 30 years. "Many of these students eat enough fat in one meal to last three days, and then we wonder why they're so lethargic."

Studies prove that Bennett's concerns are not misplaced. "A lack of physical activity has resulted in American children becoming more obese since the 1960s," reports the Educational Resources Information Center in "School Children and Fitness: Aerobics for Life." The report cautions that "this increase in body fat is responsible for reduced cardiovascular capacity which in turn limits a child's ability to resist coronary heart disease. In addition, a lack of physical activity accounts for a host of diseases including hypertension, diabetes, impaired tolerance for heat, and various psychological disorders...As children become older, there is a strong tendency for them to participate less in physical activity. The drop in such participation between the ages of 12 and 18 is dramatic." [1]

Additional reports confirm that the percentage of overweight children is increasing. A "National Health and Nutrition Examination Survey" conducted from 1988 through 1994 by the Centers for Disease Control shows that approximately 14 percent of children ages

[1] Hinkle, Scott J. "School Children and Fitness: Aerobics for Life." *ERIC Digest*, December 1992.

12-17 are overweight—an increase of six percent from 1980 to 1994.[2] A *Shape Up America!* poll, commissioned by former U.S. Surgeon General C. Everett Koop, documented the decline in activity levels among Americans of all ages: "Physical activity—which has been shown to prevent and manage such life threatening diseases as heart disease, hypertension, and diabetes—is one of the most consistent and positive forces associated with successful weight management. But data from the recent Surgeon General's Report on Physical Activity and Health indicates that 25% of American adults are not getting any exercise at all; another 40% are nearly sedentary." The findings also indicate that "teens and children are less active today than they were a decade ago," and that nationwide there is a "general attitude of complacency about children's activity levels."[3]

"When the students come in and begin to learn the basic elements of health and nutrition," Bennett notes, "they begin to make changes. And when they can enjoy a variety of sports and recreational activities in safe, well-equipped, air conditioned facilities, they begin to look forward to it. It's so important to teach kids to like exercise. For example, requiring that kids run as a punishment sends the wrong message. We do need to have discipline and structure in the program to ensure safety, but we need to make it fun.

"We also try to encourage kids to take what they learn here about exercise and share it with their families," Bennett adds. "Many parents today are afraid to let their children go outside to play, and that's had an impact on their physical fitness. We encourage them to get out with their families and walk or ride bikes. I'm a preacher when it comes to health, and I want it to stay with them for life."

[2] U.S. Health and Human Services' Centers for Disease Control. *Morbidity and Mortality Weekly Report*, March 6, 1997.

[3] *Shape Up America!* Survey on Physical Activity in the U.S., May 1995.

DISCOVERY MIDDLE SCHOOL; GRANGER, INDIANA

"Our program—and our facilities—are very progressive," says Sheila Toth, physical fitness instructor at Discovery Middle School. "The facilities allow us to present an integrated fitness/health curriculum. Our program is nothing like the 'gym class' of years ago. Kids hated it, and it was stressful. Our whole focus is training for life."

The physical fitness area at Discovery Middle School includes a spectator gym with seating for 750, an adjacent auxiliary gym, and locker areas on a lower level; with a walking track area and fitness lab on an upper level overlooking the main gym. The fitness lab includes a training area with strength and cardiovascular conditioning machines, classroom space with operable walls, and an office.

"We spend about half the time in physical activity and the other half in classroom/discussion-type activities," says Toth. "The movable walls really help us—we can use the lab/classroom space as one room, two rooms, or three. Kids can go up there and work out on the machines for 20 minutes, and then we pull them into a classroom setting for lessons or work on their portfolios. We have a student-centered approach to instruction, in which we act more as facilitators in the classroom. The space is very curriculum-friendly."

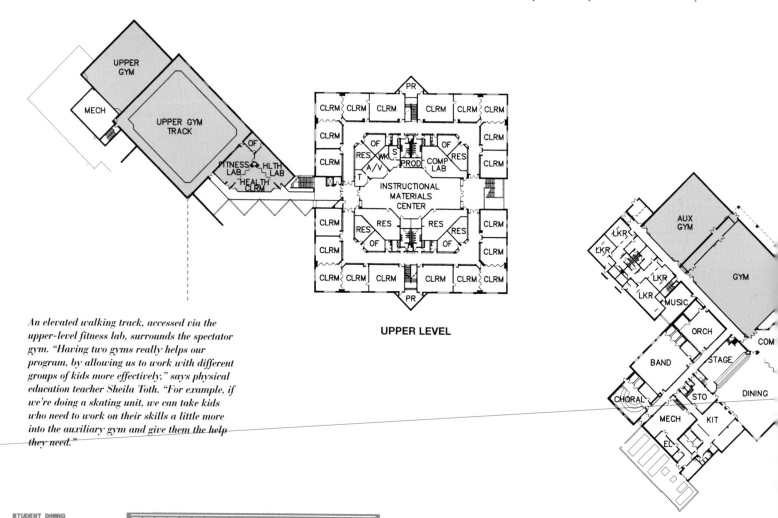

UPPER LEVEL

An elevated walking track, accessed via the upper-level fitness lab, surrounds the spectator gym. "Having two gyms really helps our program, by allowing us to work with different groups of kids more effectively," says physical education teacher Sheila Toth. "For example, if we're doing a skating unit, we can take kids who need to work on their skills a little more into the auxiliary gym and give them the help they need."

Operable walls facilitate a variety of space configurations for weight training, cardiovascular, and classroom activities at Discovery Middle School. Classroom-based curriculum units include: Diseases, Nutrition, Growth and Development, CPR/First Aid, Stress Management, Substance Abuse, and Mental and Emotional Health.

MAIN LEVEL

TRAINING FOR LIFE!

Complete a nutrition diary and a work-out journal with at least two entries a week for each. Additional journal entries should address nutrition/body system/fitness units.

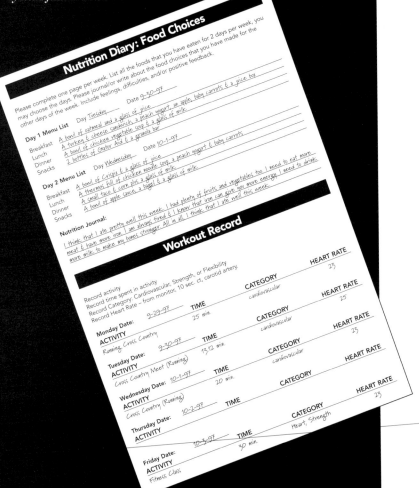

Nutrition Diary: Food Choices

Please complete one page per week. List all the foods that you have eaten for 2 days per week, you may choose the days. Please journal/or write about the food choices that you have made for the other days of the week. Include feelings, difficulties, and/or positive feedback.

Day 1 Menu List   Day Tuesday   Date 9-30-97

Breakfast A bowl of oatmeal and a glass of juice.
Lunch A turkey & cheese sandwich, a peach yogurt, an apple, baby carrots & a juice box
Dinner A bowl of chicken vegetable soup & a glass of milk.
Snacks 2 bottles of Gator Aid & a granola bar

Day 2 Menu List   Day Wednesday   Date 10-1-97

Breakfast A bowl of Crispix & a glass of juice.
Lunch A bowl of chicken noodle soup, a peach yogurt & baby carrots
Dinner A thermos full of corn plus a glass of milk.
Snacks A small taco & corn plus a glass of milk.
A bowl of apple sauce, a bagel & a glass of milk

Nutrition Journal:

I think that I ate pretty well this week. I had plenty of fruits and vegetables too. I need to eat more meat & have more iron. I am always tired & I know that iron can give you more energy. I need to drink more milk to make my bones stronger. All in all I think that I ate well this week.

Workout Record

Record activity
Record time spent in activity
Record Category: Cardiovascular, Strength, or Flexibility
Record Heart Rate – from monitor, 10 sec. ct, carotid artery.

	TIME	CATEGORY	HEART RATE
Monday Date: 9-29-97	25 min.	cardiovascular	23
ACTIVITY Running Cross Country			
Tuesday Date: 9-30-97	13.12 min.	cardiovascular	25
ACTIVITY Cross Country Meet (Running)			
Wednesday Date: 10-1-97	20 min.	cardiovascular	23
ACTIVITY Cross Country (Running)			
Thursday Date: 10-2-97		Heart, Strength	23
ACTIVITY			
Friday Date: 10-3-97	30 min.		
ACTIVITY Fitness Class			

Seventh-grade student Lissa Grashorn completed a "Nutrition Diary" and a "Workout Record" as a part of her fitness class at Discovery Middle School.

New locker rooms were added during the renovation of Thomas A. Edison Middle School in South Bend, Indiana.

A natatorium at Oak Hill Junior/Senior High School in Converse, Indiana, features a pool with a movable bottom.

Home of the Wildcats, the gymnasium at South Vermillion Middle School in Clinton, Indiana, seats 1,000 spectators.

Modernization of Thomas A. Edison Middle School incorporated a new training room for cardiovascular and strength training.

LESSONS FOR LIFE

The 10,000-square-foot main gymnasium and a smaller P.E. gymnasium at Lincoln Middle School in Indianapolis, Indiana, are housed in the public wing of the school. Large storage areas, locker rooms, restrooms, and showers divide the two gyms.

The natatorium at Wilson Middle School in Muncie, Indiana, features a six-lane, 25-yard pool. The pool is in constant use by students and the community.

Ample locker room space for boys and girls is included at Sunman-Dearborn Middle School in St. Leon, Indiana.

The renovation of Edgar Allan Poe Middle School in Annandale, Virginia, extended to the athletic fields—where playing surfaces were re-graded and re-seeded and the adjacent blacktop area was resurfaced and painted for basketball and four-square. New outdoor equipment was added as well as a perimeter fence for enhanced security.

WOOD OR SYNTHETICS?

"Re-flooring our gym floors with wood surfaces has been a big improvement for us," says Jayne Bennett, physical education teacher at Edgar Allan Poe Middle School in Annandale, Virginia. "Before, we had asphalt floors—the wood is much easier on your legs."

While wood floors—typically composed of a hard maple—are clearly best for basketball, other options, such as rubber, polyurethane, and other synthetics, are preferable for volleyball, jogging, aerobics, and many other gym activities. Many school systems must factor in community use as well as student use in weighing the decision on how to surface gym floors. Maintenance requirements should also be considered: while both wood and synthetic floors are durable, some synthetics may become slick when dusty, so custodial staff need to be able to clean the surface routinely. Although wood is more expensive, the ability to sand the floors to a new finish every few years adds to the attractiveness of this option.

Wood floors in the gymnasium are the best option for many schools, such as Bloomington Junior High School in Bloomington, Illinois.

CREATIVE EXPRESSION

"STUDENTS AT THIS AGE NEED TO QUESTION AND EXPLORE—AND THEY NEED TO EXPRESS THEMSELVES. THOSE QUALITIES ARE A GOOD FOUNDATION FOR THE ARTS."

—Dr. James J. Bird,
Superintendent,
Avondale Schools;
Auburn Hills, Michigan

CREATIVE EXPRESSION

The large chalkboard in Meridian Middle School's art room is a favorite with the students. The room features a double-sided glass display case that also faces the hallway; tables with large work surfaces, and room for easels and computers.

At Discovery Middle School in Granger, Indiana, the art room and display areas for showcasing art projects are favorites with the students. "We have a good facility for art," says Nancy LaDuke, a seventh-grade student. "Our work is on display—it's not always the most artistic, but the teacher tries to display work that shows the most effort." Eddie Beebe, also a seventh-grader, adds, "It makes you feel proud."

At an age when the world suddenly begins to seem both complex and demanding, middle school students often discover that visual and performing arts programs offer a special opportunity to explore their sense of self and their creative potential. The arts—whether singing, painting, sculpting, dancing, acting, composing music, or playing an instrument—require students to reach within and engage their own sense of self exploration and expression.

"Visual and performing arts are among the few disciplines that educate the right side of the brain," says Edmond R. Guay, a drama teacher with Avondale Schools in Michigan. "The arts touch on philosophy, intuition, and expression. Performing arts in particular encourage students to look at and feel things from a different perspective—much different from sitting at a computer, solving math problems, or reading a book. Theatre exposes kids to a whole different way of problem-solving. Self esteem is only part of it."

"We have an art show here every day, because the students' work is on display year-round," says Jan Benkoske, art teacher at Meridian Middle School in Buffalo Grove, Illinois. "It's not a once-a-year occasion. I assume that all children do their best, and every finished work should be on display." Benkoske assisted in the school's planning, and was able to contribute ideas regarding specifications for the art room in particular. "I like having glass showcases because things are protected," she says. "We do a lot of ceramics, and the students feel better knowing their work is safe."

Benkoske also points to having a separate room for the kiln as an important attribute—allowing more open space within the classroom itself and creating a safer work area. She also requested a full-length chalkboard along one wall, which is used constantly. "It's wonderful," she says. "Once you start to draw, and the kids are feeding you ideas and you're trying to brainstorm, the last thing you want to do is cram all of these things together. You just want to build and build—recognizing their ideas and including them in what you're doing. The large chalkboard really facilitates that idea."

In addition to display space, adequate lighting, and the inclusion of several sinks for clean-up, most art teachers agree that the keys to a successful art classroom are *storage* and *space*. "You could probably give me a room as big as a football field and it wouldn't be big enough," says Dale Orman, art teacher at South Vermillion Middle School in Clinton, Indiana. Still, Orman says that her art room at the community's new school is a big improvement over the previous space—bigger and lighter, with more storage and display space. "The students do much better work here," she says. "Before, we could never do sculpture, for example, because there was no room for it. But last year, with our new art room and the ability to do sculpture, we entered a competition and won every division in sculpture in our age group."

CREATIVE EXPRESSION

Similarly, music teachers point to the need for adequate space and storage—for large and small instruments, sheet music, props, and wardrobe items. Many music suites are positioned near the school's stage, and feature dressing rooms; storage closets for uniforms, robes, and costumes; music libraries; and soundproof practice and ensemble rooms nearby. Portable risers or built-in tiers in the music classrooms facilitate group practice sessions. In band rooms in particular, appropriate floor space and ceiling heights are critical to maintain an adequate—but not deafening—volume. Sinks and instrument repair areas are time-savers and help in teaching students about the appropriate care and handling of instruments.

As in other academic areas, computers are becoming integral to research, instruction, and composition in art and music, with many schools opting to include electronic music labs and

The spacious music room at the new Lincoln Middle School in Indianapolis, Indiana, helps to support an ambitious middle school music program.

The music room at North Oldham Middle School in Goshen, Kentucky, features a mirrored wall and portable risers.

portable computer stations within art classrooms. "We've got 16 music keyboards hooked to 16 computers," says Brant Moore, a band and music teacher at the recently modernized Angola Middle School in Angola, Indiana. "I'm able to do an eighth-grade music class now that is basically a composition class where they're learning to write music and put it on the computer. It's something we simply couldn't do before."

"It's our job to educate the whole student," Edmond Guay, of Avondale Schools, says. "It's important to find a way to reach them—whatever it takes—whether it's putting students in front of computer screens, putting them on the wrestling squad, or putting instruments in their hands. We need to reach them one way or another, because once a kid's brain is turned on, there's no turning it off."

A new music suite at the recently modernized Angola Middle School in Angola, Indiana, has enhanced classroom instruction and practice sessions. Classes were previously held on the school's stage.

"THE LANGUAGE OF ART"

"Art, too, is a universal language—perhaps the most evocative form of human expression. Through singing and painting and dancing, it is possible for people of different backgrounds to communicate powerfully their feelings and ideas. The arts give rise to many voices, and make it possible for people who are socially, economically, and ethnically separated to understand one another at a deeper, more authentic level. The arts help build community."

— FROM *THE BASIC SCHOOL: A COMMUNITY FOR LEARNING*[1]

The music room at A.I. Root Middle School in Medina, Ohio, features fabric-wrapped acoustical panels and built-in storage for musical instruments.

"The art rooms are very nice—what a change," says Betsy Lockman, a language arts and science teacher at Edgar Allan Poe Middle School in Annandale, Virginia. "They're nice and bright—it's amazing what light can do."

[1] Boyer, Ernest L. *The Basic School: A Community for Learning.* The Carnegie Foundation for the Advancement of Teaching. Princeton, NJ, 1995, Page 76.

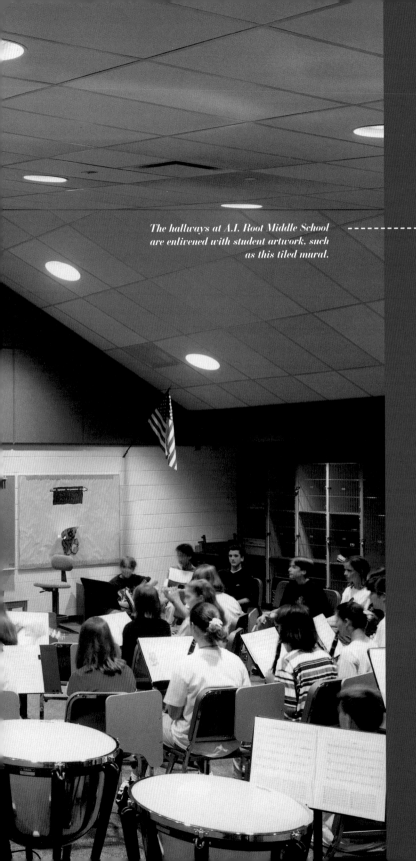

The hallways at A.I. Root Middle School are enlivened with student artwork, such as this tiled mural.

ART AND MUSIC: PHILOSOPHY AND GOALS

"Historically, every culture has given form to its feelings and ideas through art. Art is the essence of that which is human; it is the embodiment of the human experience and goal.

…To provide opportunities for educational development of middle school students, it is essential for the student to be exposed to creative experiences in art and develop an understanding of fine and applied art. The arts and crafts program of the middle school is designed to enrich the student by developing basic skills in a diverse amount of art related areas that will enhance his or her ability to express aesthetic and/or emotional feelings and ideas.

…We believe that music as an expressive art contributes to the total development of the child—emotionally, intellectually, aesthetically, and physically…music in a positive environment promotes self-esteem, fosters self-expression and facilitates creative problem solving by performing, listening, creating, studying and analyzing."

—FROM THE EDUCATIONAL SPECIFICATIONS FOR THE NEW LINCOLN MIDDLE SCHOOL, INDIANAPOLIS, INDIANA

Design of Avondale Middle School in Rochester Hills, Michigan, was a community affair. Members of the Design Review Committee included school administrators, teachers, parents, students, and school board members. Constructed to house 600 students in the seventh and eighth grades, Avondale Middle School incorporates many state-of-the-art academic and public areas that support a team teaching approach, sophisticated technology, and extensive community use.

The most challenging aspect for the Design Review Committee was the school's dual-use auditeria. Functioning primarily as performance space, the 7,335-square-foot facility also serves as the school cafeteria—seating 350 for dining and up to 600 for performances. The auditeria is acoustically engineered; features performance sound and lighting systems; and has a multi-level, tiered floor.

Set on a 22-acre site, Avondale Middle School accommodates 600 students in a 103,000-square-foot building. Teachers, students, and parents were active in the planning process for the school.

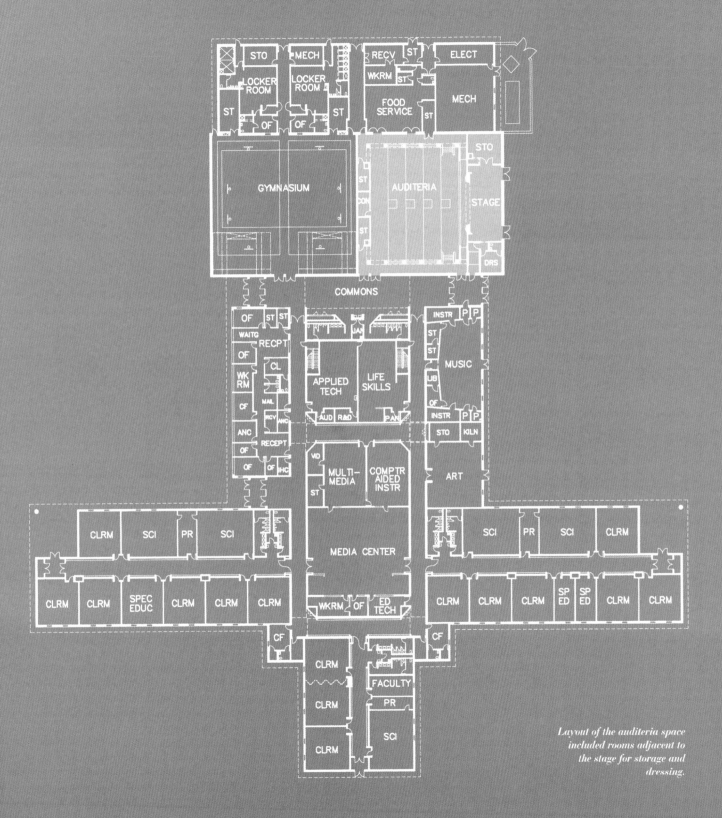

STO MECH RECV ST ELECT

LOCKER ROOM LOCKER ROOM WKRM ST

ST OF OF ST FOOD SERVICE ST MECH

GYMNASIUM ST CON ST AUDITERIA STO STAGE

DRS

COMMONS

OF ST ST INSTR P P

WAITG RECPT ST

OF CL ST MUSIC

WK RM MAIL APPLIED TECH LIFE SKILLS LIB

CF RCV ANC OF INSTR P P

ANC RECEPT AUD R&D PAN STO KILN

OF OF IHC

VID MULTI-MEDIA COMPTR AIDED INSTR ART

ST

MEDIA CENTER

CLRM SCI PR SCI SCI PR SCI CLRM

CLRM CLRM SPEC EDUC CLRM CLRM CLRM WKRM OF ED TECH CLRM CLRM CLRM SP ED SP ED CLRM CLRM

CF CF

CLRM FACULTY

CLRM PR

CLRM SCI

Layout of the auditeria space included rooms adjacent to the stage for storage and dressing.

"*An arts program is most successful when it's integrated into the curriculum. If we're building a ramp as part of a stage set, the students are using geometry. When we work on lighting, we're covering electronics. During performances, they're not just reading—they're interpreting literature. They're also learning to work in a collaborative atmosphere. But most importantly, they're developing a greater sense of self. Performing arts require risk-taking— but if they learn to get up on a stage and perform, they're also more likely to stand before a class and solve an algebra problem.*"

—**EDMOND R. GUAY, DRAMA TEACHER, AVONDALE SCHOOLS; AUBURN HILLS, MICHIGAN**

Avondale Middle School; Rochester Hills, Michigan

"That auditeria is one of the most frequently used facilities in our district," says Dr. James G. Bird, superintendent of Avondale Schools. "It's used for drama productions, musicals, awards presentations, parent meetings—all kinds of events. It's a very flexible facility that looks good, has good acoustics, and has been very durable."

"The auditeria has given our school district a performance space that is more intimate and appropriate to productions that are not as extravagant as those performed in the high school auditorium," says drama teacher Edmond R. Guay, who helped plan the facility and create the middle school's drama program. "It's a very competent theatrical venue, with

balanced acoustics and good sound, lighting, and sightlines. The space also gives our students an opportunity to learn the technical side of theatre.

"Building this auditeria validates what our students are doing in performing arts," says Guay. "It says that this district believes in the arts, and it's made people realize how important the program is."

The stage in Avondale Middle School's auditeria is used regularly by the drama class and the drama club, as well as the music programs. During the day, the space also functions as a cafeteria and a study hall—facilitated by portable tables and stacking chairs.

The auditeria at Avondale Middle School—popular for both school and community events, seats nearly 600 for performances A control room is located at the back of the facility, with follow-spot lighting bays above

CHALLENGE

"THINK LIKE AN ARCHITECT"

Study the art room in which you are now working, and think like an architect. What do you like best about this room? How could this room be even more wonderful if you could have design input?

"THE CHALKBOARD IS HUGE AND EASY FOR EVERYONE TO SEE. I WOULD MAKE ANOTHER ROOM FOR COMPUTER ARTS FOR VIRTUAL DRAWINGS."

"I LIKE THE TV AND HOW IT COMES OUT OF THE WALL. IF WE MADE IT MORE HIGH-TECH, WE COULD ADD LAPTOPS IN ALL THE DESKS AND GO ON THE WEB TO LEARN. I THINK WE SHOULD ALSO MAKE THE SCHOOL ENVIRONMENTALLY SAFE BECAUSE OF GLOBAL WARMING."

"I LIKE THE DISPLAY SHELF BECAUSE YOU CAN SEE THE OTHER PEOPLE'S WORK."

"I THINK THAT THE BEST PART OF THE ART ROOM IS THE CHALKBOARD. IT IS VERY BIG AND HAS LOTS OF ROOM. IT COULD BE BETTER IF WE KNOCKED OUT THE FIFTH-GRADE SCIENCE LAB AND MADE THE ART ROOM BIGGER."

"THE BEST PARTS OF THE ART ROOM ARE THE CEILING AND THE CABINETS. IT WOULD BE BETTER IF THEY PUT THE PAPER TOWEL DISPENSERS SOMEWHERE ELSE."

"THE BEST PART IS THAT THE ROOM HAS FOUR SINKS FOR MORE CONVENIENCE. I WOULD PUT A SPECIAL PLACE TO HOLD PAINT CONTAINERS."

"I LIKE HOW THE CEILING GOES HIGHER AND HIGHER. I WISH THE WALLS WERE PAINTED LIGHT PURPLE OR BLUE OR MULTI-COLORED."

—Assignment given by Jan Benkoske, art teacher at Meridian Middle School, Buffalo Grove, Illinois

Large sinks facilitate clean-up in the art room at Williamsburg Middle/High School in Williamsburg, Ohio.

The art room at Bloomington Junior High School in Bloomington, Illinois, is brightly lighted with tile floors, a variety of storage options, and a separate room for the kiln.

Lincoln Middle School's art room features several sinks, large work tables, and ample cabinetry and display areas.

CREATIVE EXPRESSION

The auditorium at Wilson Middle School in Muncie, Indiana, which seats 650, can be divided into three spaces for large-group instruction. The area near the stage seats 350; two sections at the back of the facility each seat 150.

The auditorium at Thomas A. Edison Middle School in South Bend, Indiana, features an operable wall that divides the facility into two sections for large-group instruction purposes.

Choir students at Hamilton Southeastern Junior High School in Fishers, Indiana, are seated on carpeted, semi-circular tiers. Flat floor space at the front of the room accommodates a piano, a podium or teacher's desk, a director's stand, and audio-visual equipment.

Central Junior High School, in West Melbourne, Florida, has a music room with a tiered floor and raised ceiling.

"Rapid Run Middle School has been planned with the needs of both students and the community in mind," says Michael J. Amos, director of operations for the Oak Hills Local School District in Ohio. The new school will include a 450-seat auditorium available for community use, and an outdoor amphitheatre and terrace.

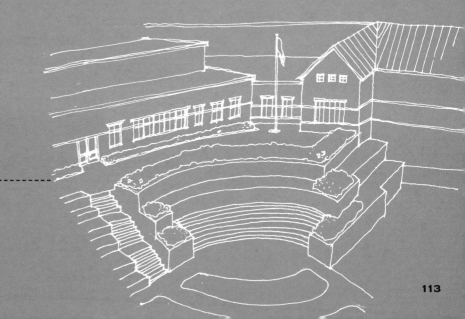

AFTER SCHOOL

"IT'S NO LONGER REALISTIC TO BELIEVE THAT SCHOOLS ONLY ADDRESS THE ACADEMIC NEEDS OF STUDENTS. IN ORDER TO CARE FOR THE 'WHOLE CHILD,' EMOTIONAL, SOCIAL, PHYSICAL, AND ACADEMIC CONCERNS MUST BE CONSIDERED. WE'VE EXTENDED OPPORTUNITIES FOR KIDS OUTSIDE OF THE REGULAR SCHOOL DAY— 8:00 A.M. TO 3:00 P.M. JUST ISN'T ENOUGH TIME!"

—Susan L. Mann, Principal, Meridian Middle School; Buffalo Grove, Illinois

HOMEWORK CLUB

INTRAMURALS

AFTER-SCHOOL PROGRAM

M/T/W/TH/F 3:15-4:30

The final bell or announcement at the end of the school day has long signaled a mad dash to the locker, a quick gathering of books and homework, and a rush out the door and onto the right bus. Today, however, more and more students are lingering beyond the last class—staying for study groups and homework clubs, after-school programs, extra computer time, intramurals, and a host of extracurricular academic and social activities.

Teachers and administrators agree that if a school stays open and active long after the end of the school day, then students are getting the right message about school in general—that it's a place to feel comfortable, secure, and at home; a place to learn and to help others learn; and a place to socialize, play, work, plan, and dream. "With our after-school program and our extended childcare program, we have kids all over this school every afternoon—until at least 6:00 p.m.," says Susan L. Mann, principal of Meridian Middle School in Buffalo Grove, Illinois. "The students learn new hobbies and skills, play in the gym, study, or just gather in the media center to read or play gin rummy. They love being here—we have all kinds of activities and events, and the school really takes on its own sense of community."

"Young adolescents do not want to be left to their own devices," reports the Carnegie Council on Adolescent Development in its 1992 report, *A Matter of Time: Risk and Opportunity in the*

NonSchool Hours. The report cites a 1988 National Education Longitudinal Study that surveyed 25,000 eighth-grade students, finding that 27 percent of the students spent two or more hours at home alone after school. Students from lower income families were likely to be left alone for three or more hours.

"In national surveys and focus groups," the Carnegie report continues, "America's youth have given voice to a serious longing. They want more regular contact with adults who care about and respect them, more opportunities to contribute to their communities, protection from the hazards of drugs, violence, and gangs, and greater access to constructive and attractive alternatives to the loneliness that so many now experience."[2]

By mid-afternoon, most middle school students still have plenty of energy, but are often easily distracted after a full day of demanding classes. The most successful after-school programs work with this energy level in mind—offering recreational sports and games and hands-on, exploratory-type activities as well as tutoring and study sessions. Some programs—such as Meridian Middle School's "After School Program," offer a number of clubs and activities—ranging from

Meridian Middle School's "After-School Program" is a lively series of clubs, classes, and recreational activities. Students register for classes that interest them; late buses help participants with transportation home.

---

[1] From "When Johnny Won't Learn," *The Washington Post,* Education Review, April 5, 1998. Page 1.

[2] *A Matter of Time: Risk and Opportunity in the NonSchool Hours.* Report of the Task Force on Youth Development and Community Programs, Carnegie Corporation of New York, Carnegie Council on Adolescent Development 1992. Page 10-11.

AFTER SCHOOL

"Paper Airplane Building," "TV Video Production," and "Gross Cooking" to "Composing Music on Computers," "Badminton," and "Gym Games"—so that students can sign up for the sessions that interest them the most.

At Angola Middle School in Angola, Indiana, even the last hour of class begins to take on an "after-school" feel, with exploratory classes offered twice a week. "The students have study hall three days a week at the end of the day, and twice a week we offer 'mini-courses,' says Language Arts teacher Scott Hottell. "Each mini-course runs six weeks, and they can choose what they're most interested in. There are a lot of games—kickball, dodgeball, frisbee golf—even hallway bowling. We've also taught hunter safety, how to tie flies for fishing, Native American games, how to make bird feeders, choral music—all kinds of things. The teachers enjoy it, because if they have an interest, they can share it with the kids. It's a great way to end the day, and the kids have a lot of fun."

At the new Crestview Middle School in Huntington, Indiana, much of the after-school program is geared toward sports and recreation. "We've expanded our intramural program because we want all kids to be able to take part," says Dr. Max F. Spaulding, superintendent of Huntington County Community School Corporation. "We offer basketball, volleyball, wrestling, weight training—we think it's important to emphasize physical activity for students. We also want to make this part of their day enjoyable—school may be over, but their parents may not be home yet. And we think it's very important to encourage kids to socialize—intramurals give them an opportunity to have fun together, instead of going home and sitting in front of the TV."

Spaulding points to the design of school buildings as being instrumental in facilitating successful after-school programs, as well as after-hours community events. "Crestview Middle School has been designed so that academic areas can be secured while students and the community can access the gymnasiums and other public areas. If the students are out playing soccer or other games, they can access the restrooms and water fountains. We want the school to be used after hours, and we want the community to use the school—it's their investment. This school will probably be open from 7:00 in the morning until 10:00 or 11:00 at night—every day."

While many students head straight for the basketball courts or soccer fields after school, other students opt for quiet time toward the end of the day—preferring study halls, homework clubs, computer sessions, visits to the media center, or one-on-one interaction with their teachers. Just as well-equipped gymnasiums and playing fields provide students with a venue for sports and recreation that they won't find at home, classrooms, labs, and media centers offer the resources many children seek for researching reports, catching up on homework, or completing assignments. Some are simply drawn to quiet areas that they may not find at home.

"My happiest time of day is after school, when the kids come back in for extra help," says Natasha Heny, an eighth-grade English teacher at Edgar Allan Poe Middle School in Annandale, Virginia. "If I didn't have a comfortable space, they wouldn't want to come. I look around and see all of the students staying to study after school and I think, 'Something's working here.'"

"By any standards, America's young adolescents have a great deal of discretionary time. Much of it is unstructured, unsupervised, and unproductive for the young person. Only 60 percent of adolescents' waking hours are committed to such essentials as school, homework, eating, chores, or paid employment, while fully 40 percent are discretionary."

—A MATTER OF TIME:
RISK AND OPPORTUNITY
IN THE NONSCHOOL
HOURS[4]

"Our new intermediate school has enabled us to start a latchkey program, called the Growing, Learning, and Developing Center, or GLAD. The way the building is designed allows the after-school students to access the gym, cafetorium, art room, music room, stage, and media center without interrupting the teachers and the custodians in the academic wing."

—Hank Smith, Superintendent,
Celina City Schools, Ohio

[3] *A Matter of Time: Risk and Opportunity in the NonSchool Hours.* Report of the Task Force on Youth Development and Community Programs. Carnegie Corporation of New York. Carnegie Council on Adolescent Development 1992. Page 9.

[4] *Ibid.* Page 10.

MERIDIAN MIDDLE SCHOOL; BUFFALO GROVE, ILLINOIS

ELEC | MECH | GYMNASIUM | CLASSROOM | COMPUTER | MEDIA CENTER | WK RM | STOR | SCIENCE | WK RM | CUST | MECH | ART

From early in the morning, when "Sniffles" and "Ozzie"—the school parakeets—greet students and teachers, until well into the evening, Meridian Middle School is bustling with activity. The school has several celebrated after-school programs—including an award-winning recreational program called "Lighted Schoolhouse"—that have become models for other districts.

While Sniffles and Ozzie may spend more time in the school than anyone else, they are joined by many students and teachers long after the regular day of classes is over. "We have an extended afternoon childcare program called 'Club Meridian,'" says Principal Susan L. Mann. "It's administered by the school and stays open until 6:00 p.m. We also have our 'After-School Program,' which is a series of courses that the students can sign up for. Some of the sessions are centered around

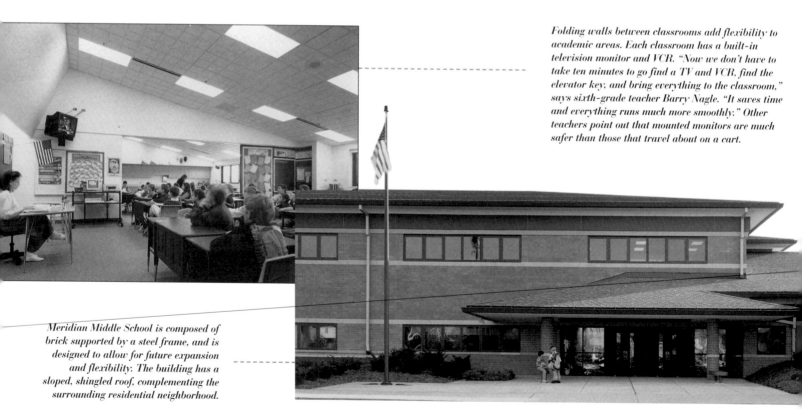

Folding walls between classrooms add flexibility to academic areas. Each classroom has a built-in television monitor and VCR. "Now we don't have to take ten minutes to go find a TV and VCR, find the elevator key, and bring everything to the classroom," says sixth-grade teacher Barry Nagle. "It saves time and everything runs much more smoothly." Other teachers point out that mounted monitors are much safer than those that travel about on a cart.

Meridian Middle School is composed of brick supported by a steel frame, and is designed to allow for future expansion and flexibility. The building has a sloped, shingled roof, complementing the surrounding residential neighborhood.

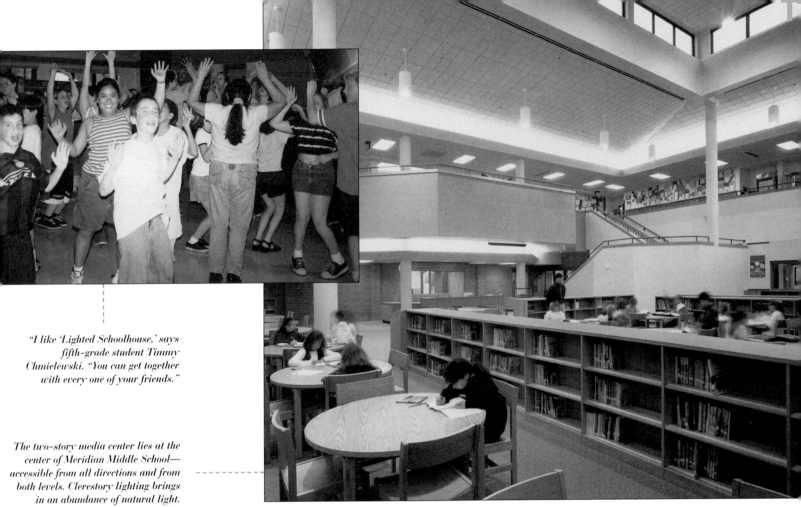

"I like 'Lighted Schoolhouse,' says fifth-grade student Timmy Chmielewski. "You can get together with every one of your friends."

The two-story media center lies at the center of Meridian Middle School—accessible from all directions and from both levels. Clerestory lighting brings in an abundance of natural light.

hobbies and games, such as chess or building model rockets. Others are more academic—computer skills, the homework club, or our news writers club. Many of the kids sign up for the sports-type activities, so we also have gym games, floor hockey, basketball—even line dancing."

The design of Meridian Middle School easily accommodates the extended use, including access by parents, volunteers, and the community after hours. Built on two levels, the 80,000-square-foot school houses 650 students in grades five and six. A carpeted, open area with built-in risers overlooks the media center; and often hosts plays, storytelling activities, and independent reading for the students. "I find the upstairs riser area very useful,"

says Sherrie Cummins, a fifth-grade teacher. "It's great for big groups, but it's also nice just to send kids out to work on their own. They love it—they think going out to the risers is the most exciting thing."

Other components of the school that support after-hours use include a large, multi-purpose room often used by parents and volunteers. "We work in partnership with parents," says Mann. "We have over 300 parents signed up to do different things."

Energy-efficient design also facilitates extended use of the school. A multi-staged chilling system optimizes energy consumption and yields low utility costs. A weather station, with wind-speed and direction sensing and

temperature sensing, determines the amount of heating required at any given time and the optimum time to start the heating and cooling system.

For the students, the after-school programs are clearly a highlight. "We hold 'Lighted Schoolhouse' one evening a month," says Mann. "We bring in a DJ and play age-appropriate music; and have dancing, games, videos, and snacks. The kids love it." The "After-School Program," with its variety of clubs and classes, has also been a hit with the students: "When I go home, all I do is turn on the TV," says Jeremy Rose, a sixth-grade student. "But the after-school classes give me something to do and I enjoy it."

AFTER SCHOOL

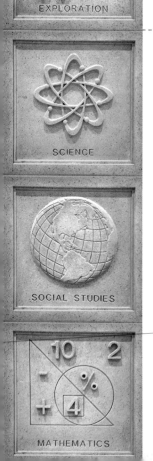

LANGUAGE ARTS

PHYSICAL EDUCATION
ATHLETICS

EXPLORATION

SCIENCE

SOCIAL STUDIES

MATHEMATICS

"At Crestview Middle School, we incorporated cast stone symbols—representing aspects of our educational program—across the front of the stage," says Dr. Max F. Spaulding, superintendent of Huntington County Community School Corporation in Indiana. "In addition to the traditional academics such as math and language arts, we included our exploratory focus and physical education, because we wanted the symbols to be reflective of all of the areas of our middle school program."

Television studios in many middle schools are typically in use before and after school for student-sponsored productions.

Computer labs are often open to students and teachers for after-school instruction and keyboarding practice.

Lecture halls and large-group instruction areas often host after-school meetings, debate and drama clubs, and awards ceremonies.

Q

"WHAT WAS YOUR FIRST IMPRESSION— AFTER LEAVING YOUR OLD SCHOOL BUILDING AND WALKING INTO THIS NEW ONE FOR THE FIRST TIME?"

A

"WE GOT GOOSEBUMPS."

"WE HAD WAITED SO LONG AND WE HAD WORKED VERY HARD TOWARD THIS AND IT WAS THE CULMINATION OF A LOT OF HARD WORK AND DETERMINATION. YES—GOOSE-BUMPS WOULD BE ACCURATE."

"I THINK A LOT OF US ALMOST TEARED UP, DIDN'T WE? I REMEMBER THAT—WE WERE REALLY EMOTIONAL."

"FOR MOST OF OUR FIRST YEAR HERE, IT DIDN'T SEEM TO SINK IN THAT WE WERE REALLY HERE AND WE WERE GOING TO STAY HERE—THAT IT WAS REALLY OUR BUILDING. IT WAS LIKE A BIG DREAM WE WERE LIVING IN—AS IF WE WERE GOING TO WAKE UP ONE MORNING AND BE BACK IN THAT OLD BUILDING. IT WAS HARD TO BELIEVE."

"IT'S JUST A DIFFERENT MINDSET TO HAVE BEEN THERE, AND NOW TO BE HERE."

"WE HAD SO MUCH PRIDE AND SATISFACTION."

"WHEN WE WALKED IN THE FIRST TIME, WE WERE SPEECHLESS. AND IT'S PRETTY UNUSUAL FOR US TO BE SPEECHLESS."

—TEACHERS AT SOUTH VERMILLION MIDDLE SCHOOL IN CLINTON, INDIANA. THE NEW SCHOOL OPENED IN 1995.

APPENDIX

SHAPING THE FUTURE
Middle Schools

Photography

The majority of professional photography that appears in this book was taken by David Emery of Columbus, Ohio. This includes the large and small photos on the front cover.

Additional credits are as follows:

Avondale Middle School: Hedrich-Blessing

Meridian Middle School: Hedrich-Blessing

North Oldham Middle School: Mike Tuell, Photo Tech, Inc.

Sunman-Dearborn Middle School: ARTOG Architectural Photography

Woodridge Middle School: North Light Studio

Meridian Middle School students - pages 5 and 121: courtesy of Susan Mann, Meridian Middle School

Lincoln Middle School students - pages 15 and 22: courtesy of Myron Cochran, Lincoln Middle School

Lockers and t-shirt - pages 18, 19, and 71: Joseph Romeo Photography

Stock market, roller coaster, Great Wall of China - pages 41, 46, and 47: FPG International

A.I. Root Middle School students - pages 44 and 45: courtesy of William Nettles, A.I. Root Middle School

Angola Middle School students - page 53: courtesy of Angola Middle School

Andrew Satten cooking photos - page 83: courtesy of Andrew Satten and family, Edgar Allan Poe Middle School

A special thank you to the following students of Edgar Allan Poe Middle School, who were photographed by Gary Landsman of Landsman Productions for the chapter title pages:

Chapter 1   DeAundra Heatley, Grade 6

Chapter 2   Michael Frost, Grade 8

Chapter 3   Shelley Selim, Grade 8

Chapter 4   Claudia Portillo, Grade 7

Chapter 5   A.J. Hill, Grade 7

Chapter 6   Sothary Heang, Grade 7

Chapter 7   Keith Nolan, Grade 8

Chapter 8   Adam Pruitt, Grade 7

Appendix   Eric Shinn, Grade 7

Text: C.L. Taylor, Capstone Communications

Design: Capital Design, Inc.

Printing: Fannon Color Printing